Gadchick F

A Beginners Guide to Using Mac OS X (10.10) Yosemite

A Guide to Unplugging You Windows PC and Becoming a Mac User

By Katie Morris

Putting the Geek in Chic

www.Gadchick.com

Cover Image © jay clark - Fotolia

© 2014. All Rights Reserved.

Table of Contents

INTRODUCTION **5**

INSTALLATION **8**
   OS X 10.9 MAVERICKS 9
   OS X 10.8 MOUNTAIN LION OR BELOW 10

SWITCHING FROM WINDOWS PC TO MAC **12**
   WHY CHOOSE MAC? 13
   MAJOR DIFFERENCES BETWEEN OPERATING SYSTEMS 17
   TRANSFERRING YOUR INFORMATION 20

THE BASICS **23**
   YOUR DESKTOP 24
   GESTURES 27
   FINDER 30
   LAUNCHPAD 31
   CONNECTING TO THE INTERNET 33
   NOTIFICATIONS 35
   SAFARI 37
   MAIL 39
   CONTACTS 43
   CONTINUITY 45
   CALENDAR 47
   REMINDERS 50
   NOTES 54
   MESSAGES 56
   FACETIME 60
   ITUNES 61
   APP STORE 70

CUSTOMIZING YOUR MAC **75**
   GENERAL 77
   DESKTOP & SCREEN SAVER 79
   MISSION CONTROL 83
   DOCK 84
   SOUND 85
   USERS & GROUPS 87
   PARENTAL CONTROLS 93
   ACCESSIBILITY 102

PRIVACY AND SECURITY **107**
   CREATING STRONG PASSWORDS 108

FIREWALL 110
FIND MY MAC 111
PRIVACY 113

MAINTENANCE **116**
PRESERVING BATTERY LIFE 117
ICLOUD 119

CONCLUSION **122**

Introduction

Apple Maps. Robert Downey Jr. Detroit. These are a few examples of great things that just exploded after some hard work and a fresh new look. After OS X Mavericks was met with indifference, many worried that future OS X updates would continue to be a steady stream of minor upgrades and tweaks. Continuing the new naming convention of Californian locations, the new iteration will be dubbed 'Yosemite' after California's beloved national park, with no relation to a certain Looney Tunes character. With OS X Yosemite, Apple is showing the world that OS X is not doomed to incremental upgrades, and diligently went through everything "feature by feature, pixel by pixel" to create a totally new and improved makeover for an old friend. If you've used any OS X version before, there's no way you'll feel totally lost as you forage through Yosemite but your computer will definitely look and feel like a brand new system.

There are many new changes both aesthetic and mechanical, and this guide will take you through it all whether you're an OS X spring chicken or a grizzled Mac veteran. If this is your first Apple computer (congrats on making the jump by the way!), we will also detail how to switch everything over from your old PC, and show you the differences between Windows and Mac. If you are ready to learn the ins and outs of OS X Yosemite, grab a fresh cup of coffee (decaf if it's late) and let's get to work.

Installation

OS X 10.9 Mavericks

First thing's first. To begin using OS X Yosemite, you actually need to have it installed. If you are already running the latest version of OS X Mavericks, pat yourself on the back and consider your job done; all you need to do now is head over to the App Store, search for OS X Yosemite, and download it. The file is just over 5 GB in size so it will take a little bit to download. Once it's finished downloading, follow the on-screen prompts. To complete installation, your Mac will restart several times. You'll know when it's finished because everything will look a lot different, you'll have cool new wallpaper, and a Welcome dialogue box will appear.

OS X 10.8 Mountain Lion or Below

If you are one of the eight Mac users that haven't yet upgraded to OS X Mavericks and are still using OS X Snow Leopard, Lion, or Mountain Lion, you will have to finally bite the bullet and click the download link for Mavericks.

On the other hand, if you are using anything less than Snow Leopard, you might need to wipe the dust off the serial number and verify that your computer will be able to handle OS X Mavericks and Yosemite.

The general requirements are:

- At least 2 GB RAM or more
- At least 8 GB of available hard drive storage
- iMac 2007 or later
- MacBook 2009 and later
- MacBook Pro 2007 or later
- MacBook Air 2008 or later
- Mac Mini 2009 or later
- Mac Pro 2008 or later
- Xserve 2009 or later

Switching from Windows PC to Mac

Switching from Windows PC to Mac

Why Choose Mac?

If you are a longtime Windows PC user and haven't had the opportunity to use a Mac, or haven't been able to spend enough time with it, you may be wondering – why choose a Mac anyway?

You may have heard many different things from Mac fans, maybe that Macs don't get any viruses, are harder to hack, have great looking apps, make your Starbucks coffee more delicious, and are overall more powerful machines. These are all true to an extent, but it goes beyond that.

Fewer Viruses

A common misconception is that Apple computers are safer because it's impossible to get viruses, unlike a Windows computer where viruses seemingly install themselves when you're not looking. While it's true that Macs are indeed safer, they can still get viruses and malware. Mac viruses are not as common, however, simply because more people have Windows computers than Macs. Apple computers only take up close to 7 percent of the market share for computer users, while Windows makes up a whopping 90 percent, which translates to far more potential targets for hackers and malicious software creators.

Straightforward Approach to Tasks and Computing

Apple's design philosophy is to just make it work simply and beautifully. This philosophy is seen across all of their iPhones, iPods, iPads, and Mac computers. The native Apple programming language is designed to get the most out of hardware, and to focus on the specific task at hand. The Mac operating system was created to be lightweight, and things work how they should. It's clean and stable. Apple develops most of the hardware and drivers needed to run everything smoothly, and you will rarely encounter a bug or crash. Goodbye, Exception Errors and the dreaded Blue Screen of Death!

With Yosemite especially, Apple has worked hard to make sure each and every built-in application is a polished, functional tool that you will actually want to use. Apps like Mail, Calendar, Messages, and Contacts are just a few examples of how Apple goes above and beyond. While Windows computers will come with some of this software out of the box, it is usually very ugly, harder to use, and forgetful. When is the last time you actually used the Windows calendar feature?

Big Focus on UI

As you can probably guess by now, Mac is much better looking than Windows. Compared to the Windows operating systems, OS X is sleek, sexy, and fast. Animations are smooth, gesture controls (more on that later) provide easy navigation, and applications look great. Where Windows has you navigate through tree controls and the ribbon (the large menu at the top of programs with all the buttons), OS X has just one thin navigation menu at the top where you can find everything by searching through the pull down menus.

No Bloatware

One of the best examples of the difference in philosophy between Microsoft and Apple is when you first purchase a computer from either company.

If you buy a Windows PC, more than likely you will have to go through several processes: set up Windows, install and update drivers, set up the Wi-Fi network, create a home network, accept or decline antivirus software that came bundled with your PC, disable several other trials of software that you'll never be interested in spending a penny on (including that pesky Best Buy bloatware and all of those free games), and *maybe*, just maybe, you'll be able to start using your new PC after an hour. Phew!

On Macs, just turn your compute on for the first time, create a user account, set up Wi-Fi, log into an iTunes or iCloud account if you have one, and that's it! No free trials, no pre-installed antivirus, no long-winded set ups. From start to finish, the Mac setup will take you all of 10 minutes if you forgot your home network's Wi-Fi password again and need to figure it out.

Keyboard and Trackpad
Whether you own a MacBook, iMac, or any other Apple computer, you will be treated to one of the best keyboards on the market. The chiclet keys are perfectly spaced out, the MacBook Pro's keyboard comes with built-in backlit illumination, and typing gives off that sweet, satisfying, not-too-loud clicking sound.

The trackpad comes on all of the MacBooks, and it's an optional peripheral for the iMacs and Mac Minis in place of a standard mouse or the Apple Magic Mouse. It is consistently rated as one of the best trackpads found on any computer, and after a brief period of use you'll see why. It's smooth, accurate, and well made, while similar trackpads on Windows laptops feel cheap and flimsy. It is also capable of handling multi-touch gestures, as you will soon learn about.

Major Differences between Operating Systems

Coming from a Windows computer, there are several differences that might be jarring to the first-time Mac user.

Right Click

As silly as it may sound, one of the biggest things you'll notice almost immediately is that there is no right-click function by default. If you feel that having a right-click function is absolutely vital, there are several ways to enable it on OS X. To bring up the alternate menu (basically what right-click is used for), you can just press and hold the Control key and click wherever you'd like to perform the right-click function.

Alternatively, you can go to System Preferences>Trackpad and check "Secondary Click". The dropdown list will allow you to select how to activate the secondary click: click in bottom right corner, bottom left corner, or click with two fingers. Experiment with these settings to determine what is most comfortable for you, but if you've used a Windows laptop before, the right corner secondary click will make you feel right at home.

Of course, if you already have a mouse you'd like to use from a previous computer, you can just plug it into the USB port and OS X will automatically map the left and right click to the appropriate buttons. During the course of this guide, you may read instructions that say right-click something; when you read this, you can use either right-click or the Control + click methods.

Keyboard Shortcuts

Where Windows computers typically have many different keyboard combinations using different keys, the Mac typically uses the Command (⌘) key. For example, if you wanted to copy, cut or paste something, on a PC you would press Control(Ctrl)+C to Copy, Ctrl+X to Cut, and Ctrl+V to Paste. On a Mac you would press Command+C to Copy, Command+X to Cut, and Command+V to Paste.

To switch between running applications on a PC, you would hold Alt and press the Tab key to cycle through programs. On a Mac, you would hold down Command and likewise press the Tab key to cycle through applications.

On your Mac keyboard, you will also notice a few strange buttons. The first one, which looks like this:
[photo of expose on keyboard)

is called the Mission Control button and is located on the F3 key. Pressing it brings up a great-looking overview of all running applications. To switch applications while in the Mission Control view, you can either click on the appropriate window, or just hover the mouse over the window and press the Exposé key again.

The other button to take note of is the Launchpad button:
[photo of Launchpad button]
that is located on F4. Pressing it will bring up the Launchpad, where you will be able to open up other applications on a whim.

There are a few other major differences between the two operating systems, but it won't be as steep of a learning curve as you may have originally thought. For every Windows tool you've used, there is a Mac counterpart. Windows has Explorer, the Start Menu, the task bar, and ribbon; Mac OS X has Finder, the Dock, Launchpad, and top navigation menu.

Transferring your Information

If you've owned a Windows your whole life, you may have tons of documents and files that you need to keep when moving over to a Mac. You can use the PC Data Transfer Service at your closest Apple Retail Store, but you may find yourself waiting a while if you haven't set an appointment.

Luckily, Apple has made it easy to do it in the comfort of your own home by providing a tool called Migration Assistant. Before continuing with the migration, make sure both computers are turned on and connected to the same network, either through Wi-Fi or Ethernet cable. You can also connect the two computers by using a single Ethernet cable plugged into both computers' ports.

1. On your PC, search for the Windows Migration Assistant download link on the Apple.com website, and install it. Open the program, click Continue, and switch to your Mac.

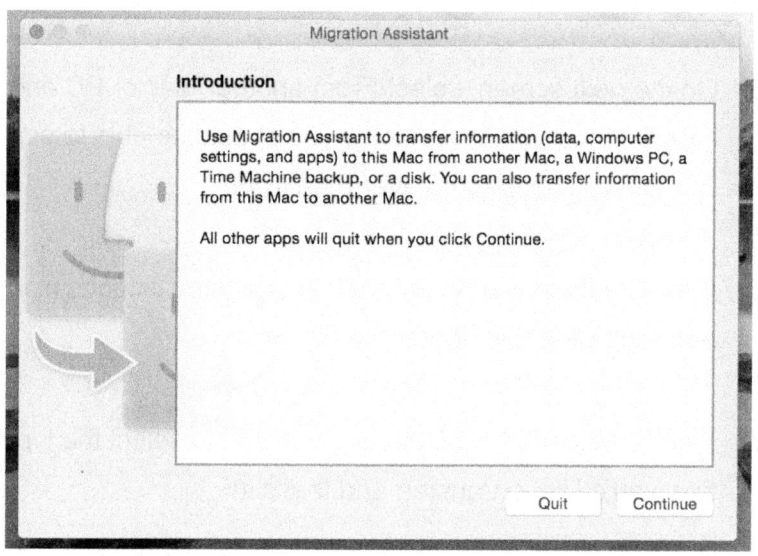

NOTE: Before proceeding, make sure you don't need any other windows open. Migration Assistant will shut down all running applications and log you out in order to continue.

2. On the Mac, open the preinstalled Migration Assistant by going to Launchpad>Other and clicking the icon. You may be asked to type in your user password to continue. The screen may turn black for a brief moment as all of your applications are closed, and the Migration Assistant screen will come up.

3. Click Continue, and on the following screen, select "From another Mac, PC, Time Machine backup, or other disk".

4. Select Continue, and enter your user name and password again if prompted.

5. On the next screen, select From another Mac or PC and click Continue. In the window you should be able to see the PC that you need to transfer data from.

6. Click Continue, verify on the PC that the passcodes match, and click Continue again.

7. Finally, Migration Assistant will ask you to select the types of files you'd like to transfer, and that's it!

Manual migration is always an option if you prefer to do things the hard way. You could do this a number of ways: burn data CDs on your Windows PC, store files on a cloud-based storage service like Dropbox, SugarSync, or iCloud Drive, or move your files onto an external storage device like a portable hard drive that you can move between computers.

The Basics

Now that you've completed the transfer of files from your old PC to the shiny new Mac, it's time to explore a little and figure out what's what.

Your Desktop

Desktop

The desktop is where the magic happens! Similar to the desktop on Windows, this is where you will be able to view programs that are currently active. You can organize the desktop by separating files into folders and sorting by name, type, size, date modified, and more. You'll also be able to enjoy beautiful wallpapers (or not-so-beautiful if you're a huge fan of Steve Buscemi), and screen savers.

Apple Menu

The Apple menu is a subsection of the top menu bar, designated by the little Apple logo. Like the menu bar, it is visible at all times unless an Application is in full-screen mode. The Apple menu is where you perform important tasks such as Force Quit, Sleep, Restart, Shut Down, and Log Out. You can also read an overview of your system specifications, view storage capacity, and perform system updates by clicking on About This Mac.

Menu Bar

Here is where you will be performing most of your tasks within an application. Say for example you are on Safari, caught in an endless cycle of searching for funny cat videos to watch. Since you are in the Safari application, the very first item on the menu bar (after the Apple menu) will be the word Safari in bold. This item will change to match whatever program you are in, so Microsoft Word will change it to Word, Evernote will change it to Evernote, and so on.

Clicking the item will open a dropdown menu that will provide standard functions pertaining to the open application. In the Safari example, we would have things like About Safari, Preferences, Clear History and Website Data, and Quit Safari. The rest of the menu bar is populated by common dropdown menus like File, Edit, View, Window, and Help, along with special dropdown menus related to whatever program is running.

Menulets

This little area is full of things called menulets. Aside from having a cute name, menulets serve as a quick shortcut to commonly used applications or functions. If you use Evernote or Dropbox for example, little menulets with the program's icon will appear, allowing you to quickly access your Dropbox folder or create a quick note using Evernote.

The second half of the menulet area is populated with useful built-in shortcuts like Wi-Fi connections, battery life (on MacBooks), the time, Spotlight search, and notifications.

Dock

The dock is where all of your commonly used applications, files, and shortcuts can be saved for easy access. Each item's icon is set against a translucent background, and Yosemite's new, flat design has the dock looking better than ever. When a program is running, you are notified via a little black dot directly underneath the app icon. We will go over the dock in more detail later, and show you how to get that signature "magnifying" effect that you've probably seen on other Macs.

Traffic Lights

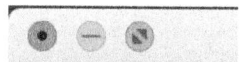

Not the official name, but these buttons are affectionately called stoplights or traffic lights by Mac users because of their color scheme and placement. The first button is a red X, which upon being pressed will close out of the current window. The yellow button, a – icon, is used to minimize the window into the dock.

The final button, green with two arrows pointing away from each other, used to be for maximizing the window without going into full screen mode. With OS X Yosemite, that button now brings the application into full screen mode, hiding everything else. If you'd still like to use the old version, you can by holding down the Option key and clicking the green button. You will notice that the arrows will now change to a + to indicate the different function.

Gestures

If you are using a MacBook, or the trackpad peripheral for your iMac or Mac Mini, you can navigate using several different gestures.

Clicking

This one is pretty simple. To perform a primary click (left click on a Windows PC), you can click anywhere on the trackpad.

Like we mentioned in the **"Major Differences between Operating Systems"** section, you can also set a secondary click (right click) to bring up the alternate menu by changing the setting in System Preferences.

Zoom

Pinch your fingers together and move them away from each other to zoom in on images and websites, or bring them closer to zoom out. If you have an iPhone or iPad, this should be very familiar as it's the same motions you use every day! You can also use Smart Zoom if you need to zoom in on a thumbnail or the website appears too small. Just hover over the area you would like to zoom in on, and double tap (don't click) twice.

Scroll

While writing documents, viewing websites, or browsing through windows, you will find yourself needing to scroll. If you are using a trackpad, there is no wheel you can use like with a computer mouse. Instead, you can scroll by dragging up or down with two fingers at the same time. If you leave the default setting ("natural", according to Apple), dragging two fingers in a downward motion will scroll up, and an upward motion will scroll down. This can be changed if you don't do well with inverted controls, as we will talk about in our **"Customizing Your Mac"** section.

Rotate

You probably won't find yourself using this one unless you are a graphic designer, photographer, or have a tendency to take pictures with an upside down camera. You can rotate images by placing two fingers on the trackpad and twisting them around. It's not really the most comfortable motion, but you do get better with practice.

Look Up

This is a pretty cool gesture, especially if you find yourself reading online often. In case you find a word you don't quite understand, like [weird word 1] or [weird word 2], you can look up everything there is to know about it by tapping on it once with three fingers.

Notification Center

To get quick access to your notifications, swipe from the right edge of the trackpad to the middle. To hide the notifications again, swipe from the middle of the trackpad to the right edge.

Show Desktop

To switch over to your desktop view, start by pinching your thumb and three fingers on the trackpad, and then spread them away from each other. Keep in mind, however, that this will only work if the application is not in full screen mode.

Switch Full Screen Applications

Working with apps in full screen mode can be cumbersome, especially if you need to keep switching back and forth. This is made even worse if you have a smaller MacBook like one of the 13" inch models. Thankfully, this gesture is very easy to use and works great. To switch between full screen apps and your desktop, just swipe either left or right with three fingers.

Mission Control

"Houston, this is Mission Control – There's a ton of gestures on this Mac!" To bring up an overview of all running applications with a gesture, slide up from the bottom of the trackpad to the middle, or slide down to exit Mission Control.

Finder

Finder on the Mac is the equivalent to Explorer on Windows. Click it to bring up a window where you can browse through the entire computer's files including applications, connected devices, documents, downloads, and iCloud Drive. You can also use the search bar to find exactly what you're looking for, or filter by tags.

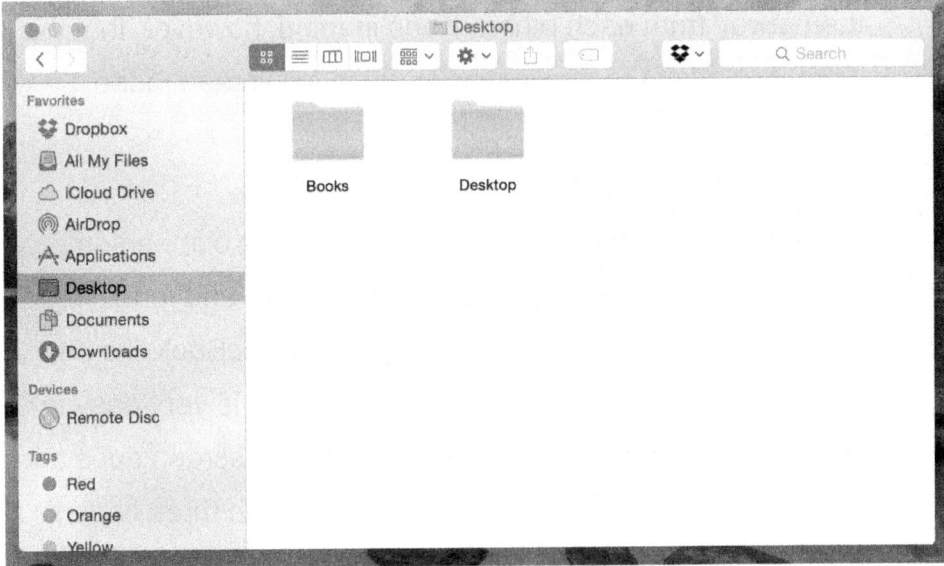

Launchpad

Launchpad is where you will be able to open up any installed applications that may not be found on the dock. Coming from Windows, this would be the equivalent to the Start Menu. As you install new applications, more pages will be automatically created to accommodate your growing collection. If you have many pages (those darned addicting Facebook games really grip you) you can easily search for a specific application by using the search bar at located at the very top.

Uninstalling Applications

If you downloaded an app that you'd no longer like on the computer, you can uninstall it in one of two ways.

Applications that were downloaded through the App Store can be uninstalled by opening up Launchpad and either holding down the Option key or clicking and holding on an icon until all of the icons start jiggling. You can tell which apps were downloaded through the App Store because they will display an X in the top left corner. Find the icon of the app you'd like to uninstall and click on the X to finish uninstalling it.

If you downloaded applications another way and would like to uninstall it, just drag the icon from Launchpad into the Trash icon in your dock.

Connecting to the Internet

If you intend to use your computer for more than just word processing, you are going to have to connect to the internet sooner or later. You can do two different ways: with a hardwired connection, or using Wi-Fi.

Setting Up Ethernet

If your computer will be stationed relatively close to your home's modem (or any modem you are near), you can create a physical connection by using an Ethernet cable. Take one end of the Ethernet cable and connect it to an appropriate port from the back of the modem or router, and plug the other end into your Mac.

Some models, like the Retina Display MacBook Pro or MacBook Air, don't include Ethernet ports so this feature would be unavailable. If that's the case, you can only connect to the internet using a wireless connection. A nice benefit of using an Ethernet cable however is that you tend to enjoy strong, stable connections where wireless networks might waiver in signal strength or connection speeds. If you absolutely need to connect using an Ethernet cable but own a computer model that doesn't have the port, you can purchase an additional adapter that converts a USB or Thunderbolt port into an Ethernet port.

Setting Up Wireless Networks

If you own one of the above-mentioned computers, or would rather connect to a network wirelessly, you can do it by clicking on the Wi-Fi menulet in the top menu bar.

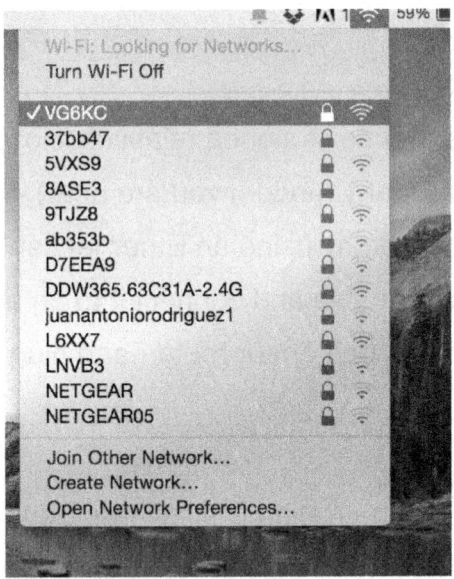

Upon clicking it, you'll notice that you can toggle between Wi-Fi On or Off. Make sure it's turned on, and the computer will automatically begin searching for the strongest wireless networks near you. The names will appear on the left while the right side will show you signal strength, and whether it's a locked network or not. If it's locked (secured), it will show a padlock icon.

36

To connect to a wireless network, click on the name and enter the password if necessary. If you don't need a password, the computer will automatically connect. If a password is required, it will authenticate your computer and the connection will be made afterwards.

Notifications

Notifications are a new feature with OS X Yosemite. In the top right hand corner you will notice a menulet that looks like three bulleted items; that is the notifications menulet. You can click it to open notifications, or if you are using a trackpad, swipe from the right edge of the trackpad to the middle using three fingers.

The notifications bar now works just like it does on iOS devices – you can switch between the Today and Notifications tabs. Today is where you'll be able to see the current date, upcoming calendar events, and widgets such as stocks or weather. The Notifications tab will show you notifications from different programs, sorted by application. If you use Facebook or Messages, for example, you will be notified each time you receive a new message or comment. The notification will appear as a small preview, and clicking on it will take you directly to the program.

Today		Notifications

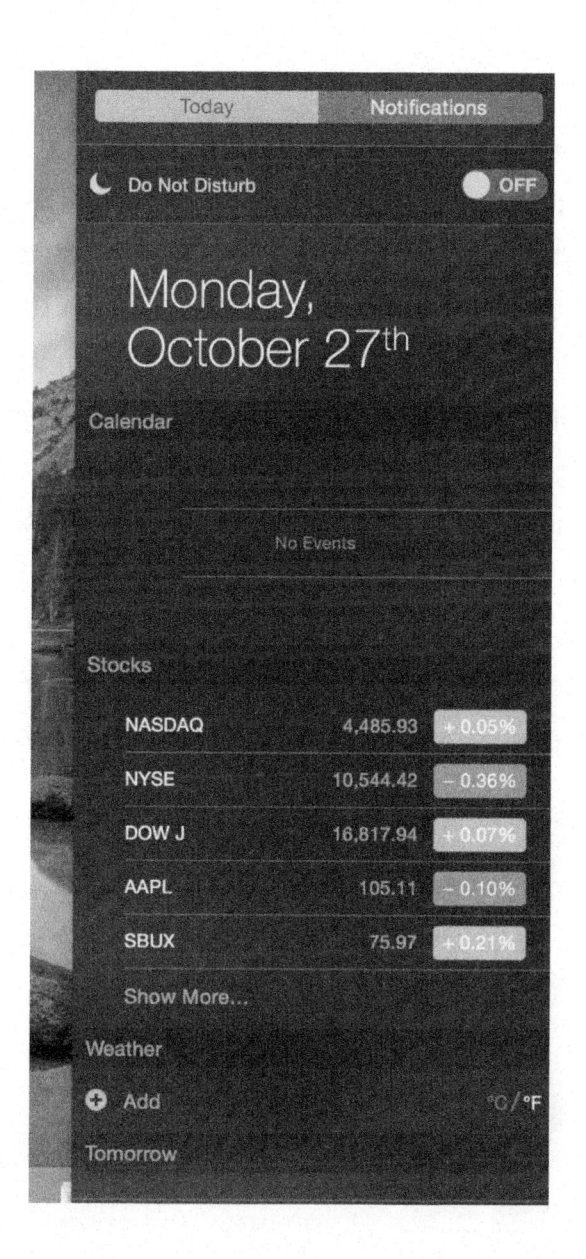

☾ Do Not Disturb　　　　　　　　　　　OFF

Monday, October 27th

Calendar

No Events

Stocks

NASDAQ	4,485.93	+0.05%
NYSE	10,544.42	−0.36%
DOW J	16,817.94	+0.07%
AAPL	105.11	−0.10%
SBUX	75.97	+0.21%

Show More...

Weather

⊕ Add　　　　　　　　　　　　　°C/°F

Tomorrow

Safari

Mac computers come standard with Safari, Apple's own web browser. While Safari has never been known for its clutter, Apple has completely overhauled the browser to have even less distractions. It's removed most of the buttons that were always visible, and left only the most important ones. From top left to right you have the standard stoplights, Back, Forward, Show Sidebar, Address Bar, Share, Tabs, and Show Downloads. After a fresh installation of Yosemite, your Safari browser will show you the standard Favorites like Apple, iCloud, Yahoo, Google, Wikipedia, and of course, Facebook. This allows easy access to the sites you visit every day.

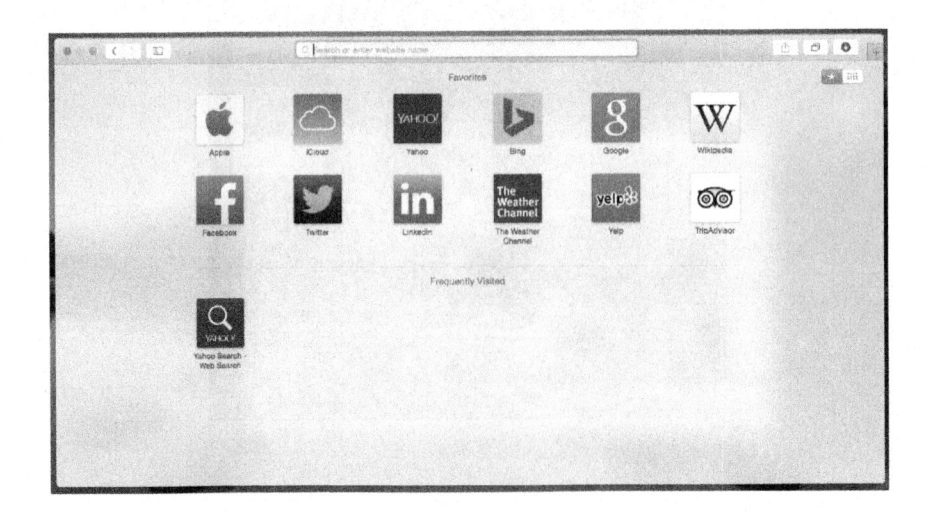

Safari works great if you tend to keep multiple tabs open. To open a new tab, you can either click on the + button at the far right of the window, or click File > New Tab. If you prefer to open an entirely new window or a private window that doesn't track search or browsing history and disables cookies, click File > New Window or New Private Window. Multiple tabs can be split up into windows by clicking and dragging the tab into an empty space.

To modify the privacy settings for Safari, skip to the Privacy section to learn more.

Mail

The built-in Mail application is a great way to keep all of your emails in one place without having to visit each individual email client's website. With the new OS X Yosemite update, the flatter design gives it a crisp, modern look.

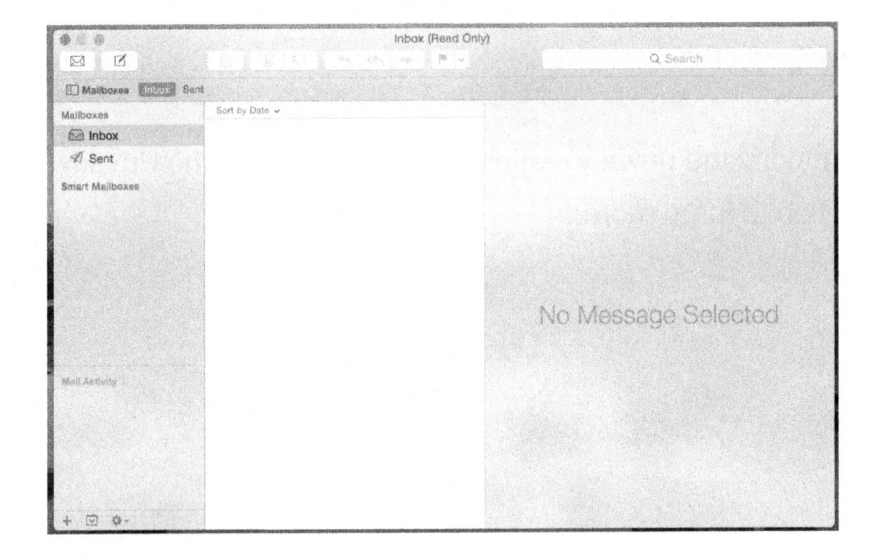

Adding Accounts

If you haven't synced an existing email account to Mail yet, let's do that first.

1. To begin, locate the Mail icon by using either Launchpad or the dock and click on it.

2. Once it's up and running, go to the menu bar and click on Mail > Add Account. The Add Account dialogue box will pop

up, prompting you to select which type of email you'd like to set up first. The biggest email providers are all here including Google, Yahoo, iCloud, and AOL. Other email addresses like those set up by your local Internet service provider can still be entered by clicking Add Other Mail Account.

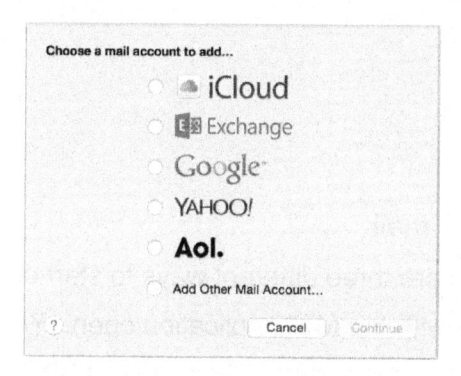

```
Choose a mail account to add...
    ○  ● iCloud
    ○  ⊞ Exchange
    ○  Google
    ○  YAHOO!
    ○  Aol.
    ○  Add Other Mail Account...
    ?                    Cancel   Continue
```

3. Click on the radio button next to the email type you want to add, and select Continue. You will be prompted to enter your iCloud email address and password if you selected iCloud. If you chose any other type of email you will be asked to enter your name as you'd like it to appear, followed by your email address and password.

43

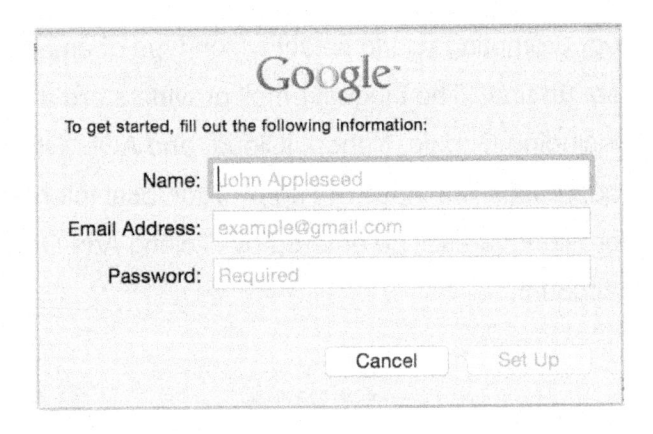

Sending an Email

1. There are three different ways to start composing a new email with the Mail application open. You can either press Command + N, select File > New Message, or click on the Compose icon (the pencil going through a square).

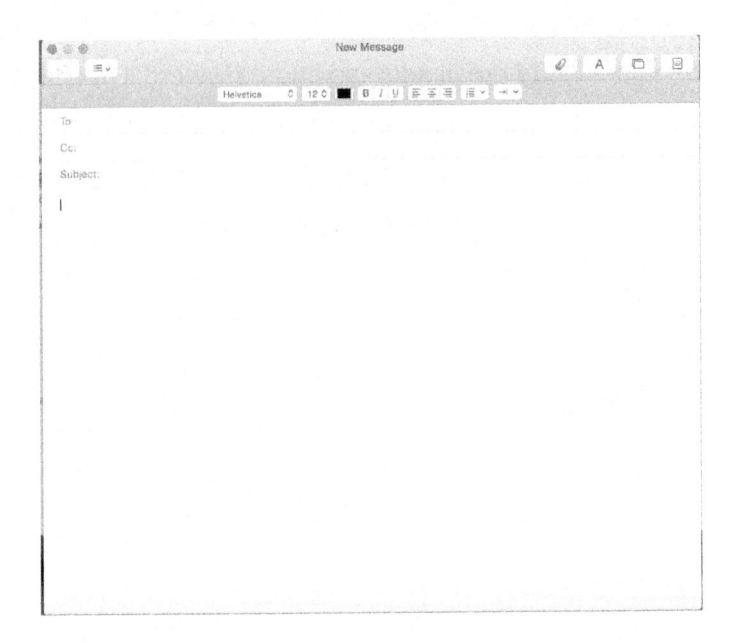

2. The New Message dialogue box will appear. In the To field, enter the email address or addresses that you'd like to send a message to.
3. In the Subject field, type a brief description of what the email is all about.

4. In the main body of the email, proceed to write anything you need to.

5. If you'd like to pretty up your text, click on the A button at the top of the window to open the Format bar.

6. If there are any files that you'd like to attach, click the paperclip icon, browse for the file, and press the blue Choose button.

7. When you're finished and ready to send the email, click the paper airplane button at the top left corner.

Contacts

You might think it's a little impractical to have a well-designed contacts program on a computer. After all, if you meet your soul mate or come across a must-have business contact, the moment would be destroyed and you'd scare everyone away if you pulled out a MacBook Pro or set up your iMac in the local supermarket just to add a new contact. Besides, doesn't your phone do it better and easier?

While it's true that the phone will always be the most convenient choice when it comes to adding contacts during day-to-day activities, OS X Yosemite brings with it a few updates to the way contacts work across your devices. Previously, you could be logged into the same FaceTime account on your iPhone, iPad or Mac and you would be able to answer video and audio calls. Though that still remains, you can take it a step further now.

Continuity was introduced for iPhones, iPads, and iPods running the latest version of iOS 8, and Macs had the feature included in the upgrade to Yosemite. It allows users to start a phone call on one device, then pause it, go to a new device, and resume the call. That means now you aren't just limited to accepting FaceTime calls on your Mac, and can call anyone your dialing finger desires.

Before we show you how to use continuity, let's figure out how to add, remove, and edit contacts first.

1. Search for the Contacts application using Launchpad or the dock. Click on it.

2. The Contacts window will open, and on the left hand side you can filter contacts by All Contacts, All iCloud, or All on My Mac. It's strongly recommended that you stick to one contact list and have everything synchronized through iCloud. If you don't have an iCloud account yet, skip ahead to our iCloud section and come back here when you're done, we'll be waiting. If you already have an iCloud account, skip to the next step.

3. To create a new contact, click on the (+) button located at the bottom of the main window. You'll be prompted to enter a new contact or a new group of contacts. Select new contact.

4. Here you can enter as much or as little information as you'd like. Things like first and last name, company name, home phone, cell phone, email, website, birthday, and home or work addresses can be entered. You can also designate different ringtones and texttones to help distinguish who's who without looking at your phone. A fun idea is to set the theme from The Omen movie as the ringtone for your boss.

5. If you need to edit a contact (or if you regret doing that ringtone idea), click on the contact name and change the field as needed, or delete the field entirely by clicking on the red delete button next to each field. To add more fields, click the (+) button again and select from Add Field to Card. A quick exploration will reveal that you can even set a nickname or maiden name for a contact!

6. To delete a contact, highlight the name of the contact you want to let go and press the Delete button on your keyboard. See ya later, Big Earl!

Continuity

Alright, so back to continuity. It's not a single specific function, but instead it's the name given to a suite of new features for OS X Yosemite and iOS 8.1+ users. Before continuing, both your iPhone and Mac must be connected to the same Wi-Fi network and logged into the same iCloud account.

You are now able to make a phone call by using your Mac (with the iPhone close by), or receive calls. To make a call from the Mac, find a number in Contacts, Safari, or FaceTime, and right-click, selecting Call with iPhone. Incoming calls will show up as a notification in the top right corner of your computer screen. You can choose to answer or decline, and if you answer, the entire call can be done without having to switch to your iPhone.

Messages can also be done through either a Mac or iPhone now. While iMessages could be synced before, the new update includes SMS text messages so you can send messages to contacts that don't have an iPhone. Additionally, the entire conversation will be viewable on both devices, so you can truly pick up where you left off regardless of which device you are using.

Finally, perhaps the coolest new continuity feature is Handoff, which lets you basically switch between devices without skipping a beat. If you are browsing a website, typing up a report, or creating a new email, you can put it down, go to your other device, and resume without having to do any searches. As long as both devices are connected on the same network and iCloud account, you will be able to see the last app used through an icon that appears on the dock for Macs, and lock screen for iPhones. Handoff is made to work with Mail, Safari, Maps, Messages, Reminders, Calendar, Contacts, Pages, Keynote, and Numbers. New applications using this feature could be rolled out soon, as developers are allowed to incorporate Handoff into their programs.

Calendar

The Calendar is another one of those applications that just looks so good with OS X Yosemite that even if you didn't use it before, you'll find yourself wanting to use it now. Find the Calendar icon in your Launchpad or dock, click on it, and let's learn how to do a few things with it.

At the top of the application window from left to right you have the standard stoplight buttons, Calendars, New Event (+), several different views including Day and Month, and the Search bar.

Syncing Calendars

If you already use a calendar with iCloud, Google, Yahoo, or any other provider, you can sync it up with the Mac Calendar application.

1. In the top menu bar click Calendar > Add Account.

2. Like you did with Mail, you'll be prompted to enter your name, email address, and password.

Once you finish the setup process your events from that calendar should automatically populate in the Calendar window. If you have multiple accounts with separate calendars, you can filter through them by clicking on the Calendars button in the toolbar, and checking or unchecking the boxes next to the appropriate calendars.

Changing Views

You can change the calendar view between Day, Week, Month, or Year by clicking on the corresponding button in the toolbar.

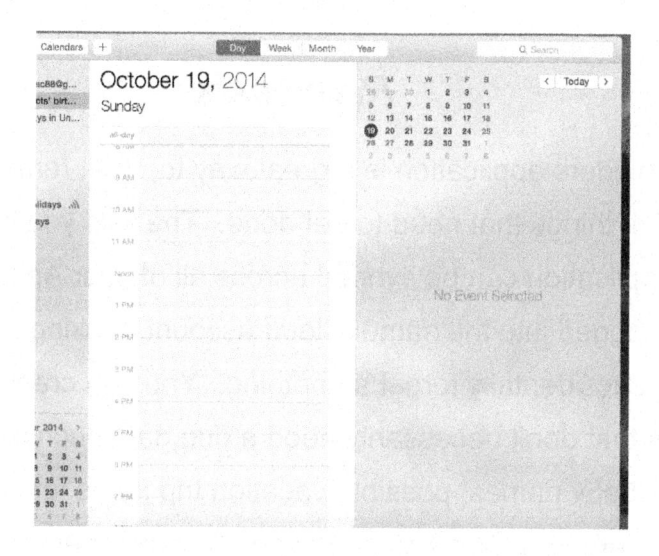

Day will display all of that day's events, broken down by hour. This view is perfect for those who have extremely busy schedules, every day.

Week will show you the whole week at a glance, and display blocks for events so you can easily see when you have events, and if you have any upcoming free time. The Week view is perfect for busy bees that have lots planned but the events are spread out over an entire week instead of just one day.

The Month view will probably be your default view if you just need your calendar to remind you about bill payments and due dates, or don't have too many appointments each month but they are scattered around. You'll see the entire month at a time, and the only event information you'll see is the title.

Reminders

The Reminders application is a great way to, well, remind yourself of things that need to get done. The lists you create in this application can be synced across all of your Apple devices logged into the same iCloud account, making sure you don't accidentally forget something. You can create lists of things that don't necessarily need a due date such as potential baby names, possible vacation trip ideas for next year, grocery lists, or home improvement ideas that you'd like to get done one day.

You can also create lists of scheduled items that have due dates and can remind you with a notification or alarm. These time-sensitive lists could have items like must-do home improvements before winter comes, reminder to pick your tomatoes and lettuce before the end of the week, or take your car for an oil change at the end of the month.

Before continuing, open up the Reminders application.

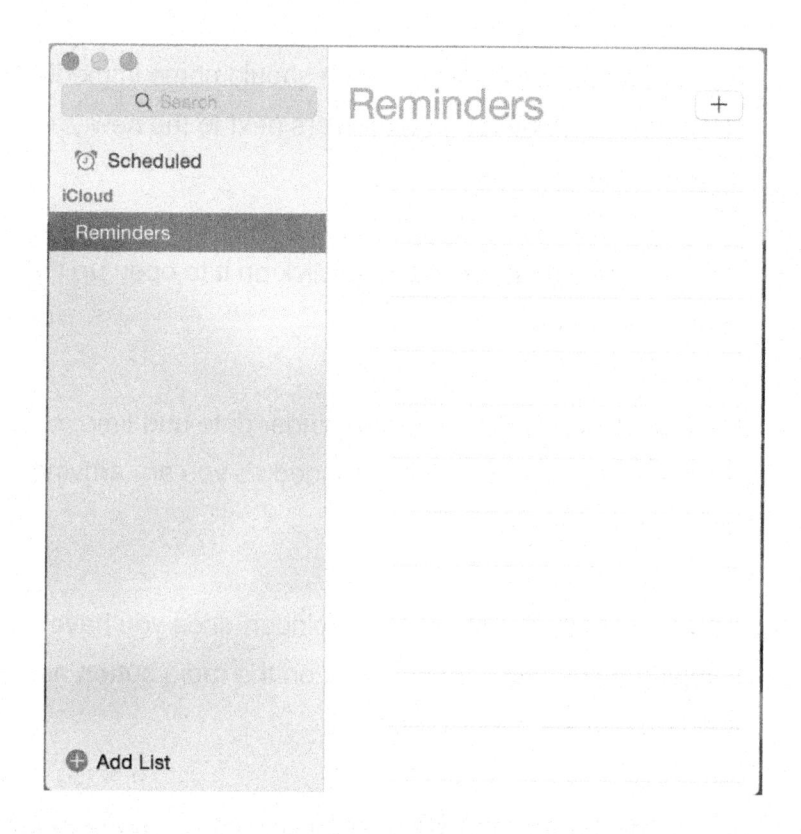

Creating Single Reminders

If you just need to be reminded of a single item, or several different items that are not related, you should enter them into the Reminders list.

1. With the application open, click on Reminders in the left hand window.

2. In the main window, click on the (+) button next to the title of the list ("Reminders" in this case).

3. A new item will be added that you should name immediately. Notice the radio button that appears next to the newly created item.

4. Once the item is named, double click on it to open up the information pane.

5. Here you'll be able to set the reminder date and time, priority level, and if you'd like to be reminded as you are arriving or leaving someplace.

6. Fast forward to the day of the reminder, once you have completed the task, you can click on the radio button next to the item to mark it as Completed.

7. You'll then be able to hide or show any previously completed items.

8. To delete items whether complete or incomplete, click on the name to highlight it and press the Delete key.

Creating New Lists

You don't have to use the default Reminders list, especially if you want to create lists without due dates. You can create your own custom lists and add as many or as little items as you wish.

1. Open up the Reminders application if you closed out of it before.

2. On the left hand side of the window, at the bottom you will see (+) Add List. Click it and enter a name for your newly created list.

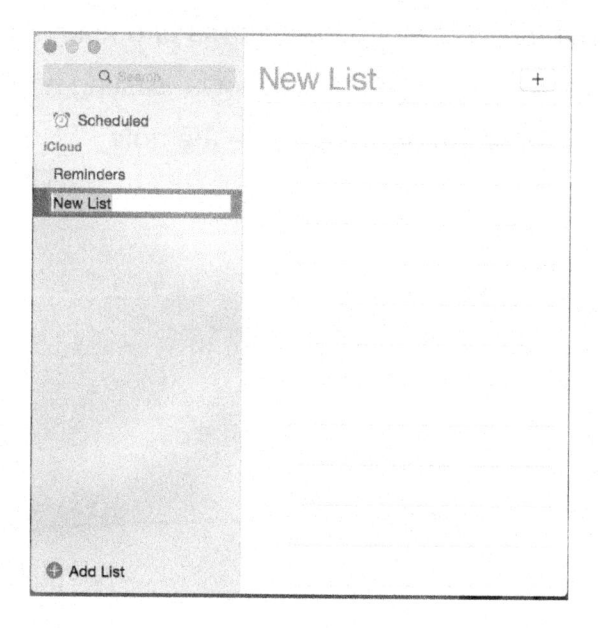

3. Once the new list is named, click on it and press the (+) button next to the list title as you did with Remainders to add new items. You can also choose whether you want due dates or not.

Notes

The Yosemite update to Notes makes it look much better, and like Safari, the unnecessary and distracting things have been omitted from view. Launch the Notes application either through the dock (if it's there), or Launchpad. Notice how there isn't much of anything in terms of a user interface. All you have is a left sidebar that shows existing notes, and a right window where you can write the note.

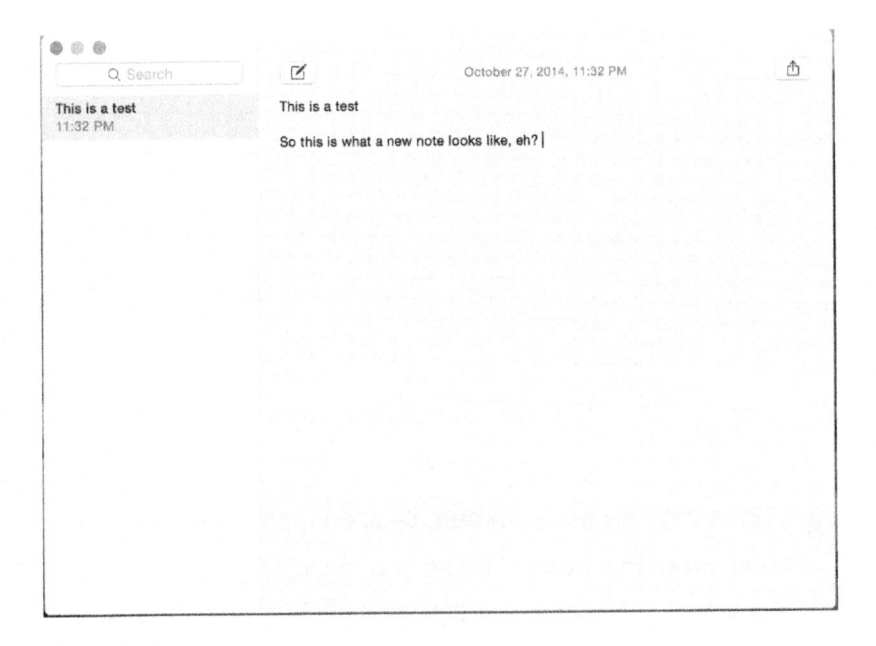

Creating and Editing Notes

1. There are a few different ways to create a brand new note. You can start a new note by clicking on the Compose icon (the square with a pencil going through it), or double clicking

an empty space in the left sidebar. You can also right-click the left sidebar and select New Note.
2. Once the note is created, the line will begin blinking in the right window, indicating that it's time for you to get writing.
3. The notes will automatically save as you type, so exiting Notes won't mean you lose progress.
4. If you need to pick up where you left off on a note, you can use the search bar to find the exact note you are looking for, or scroll through the left sidebar and select the appropriate note. With the note highlighted, click anywhere in the right window to begin editing that note, or double-click to open up a smaller window.
5. To remove notes, find the one you'd like to delete and highlight it. Press the Delete key and confirm it. You can also right-click a note and select Delete.

Notes can be shared through different outlets like LinkedIn, Facebook, Mail, and Messages. If you'd like to share a note, click on the Share button in the top right corner and select how you'd like to send it.

Messages

The Messages application is the de facto way to keep in touch with contacts while on your Mac. It's an instant messenger and iMessages all rolled into one. You can also send and receive files including photos and videos, use voice chat, and hold video chats. If you have never used an instant messenger, look around you and ask the nearest teenager to give you a quick rundown.

iMessage

If you have an iCloud account setup on the Mac, you'll be able to get in touch with friends, family, and coworkers who use Apple devices by through iMessage. The best way to think of iMessage is like an instant messaging program made specifically for the family of Apple devices (iPhone, iPad, iPod, and Mac).

There are several benefits to using iMessage:

- It uses the internet and is free so it doesn't require a text messaging plan if you are using it on a phone

- It keeps your conversations synced across all of your Apple devices as long as they are logged into the same iCloud account

- Unlike most other instant messaging programs, you can send messages to someone without them being logged in or online, and they will receive it once they get back online.

Setting Up iMessage
1. To set up iMessage, click the Messages icon to launch it.
2. If you were already logged into iCloud on the Mac, you will automically be logged into iMessage.
3. If you'd like to change this account or haven't yet logged in, select Messages > Preferences on the top menu bar.

4. When the Accounts dialogue box comes up, click on the Accounts tab.
5. In the left hand window, you will see iMessage. Select it.
6. The following screen will prompt you to enter the email address and password associated with iCloud. Do so and click the blue Sign In button to complete the setup process.

Setting Up Other IM Clients

As we mentioned, Messages is capable of mashing up your entire favorite messaging clients into one. In addition to iMessage, you can also add Google Talk, Yahoo, AOL, and many others. To add other instant messaging (IM) clients to Messages:

1. Open up Messages if it isn't already running.
2. On the top menu bar, click Messages > Add Account.

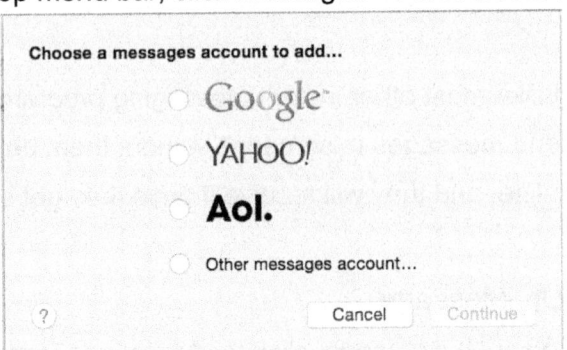

```
Choose a messages account to add...
    ○ Google
    ○ YAHOO!
    ○ Aol.
    ○ Other messages account...
                        Cancel    Continue
```

3. Select the type of account that you'd like to add, such as Gmail or Yahoo, and select Continue.
4. You will be prompted to enter the appropriate email address and password, and click the Set Up button to finish.

Now that you have iCloud or an IM client setup, let's start messaging unsuspecting friends and family!

Start New Conversation

1. Before we begin, take a look at the entire messages screen. It should be totally empty with no conversations. On the left sidebar it will say No Conversations. This is where you will be able to change between different conversations with people by clicking on each one. On the right hand side, you will also see No Conversation Selected. Here is where you will be able to type new messages and read everything in whatever conversation is currently selected. If you have an iPhone (or any phone for that matter), it will be like the screen where you read your text messages.
2. To create a new conversation with someone, click the Compose new message button located at the top of the left sidebar, next to the search bar. It should look a little pencil inside of a square.

FaceTime

FaceTime allows you to connect with friends and family using your computer's built-in camera. The app can be launched by clicking on Launchpad > FaceTime. The window will come up and your camera will turn on, letting you in on a sneak peek of what you'll look like to everyone else in case you have something stuck in your teeth.

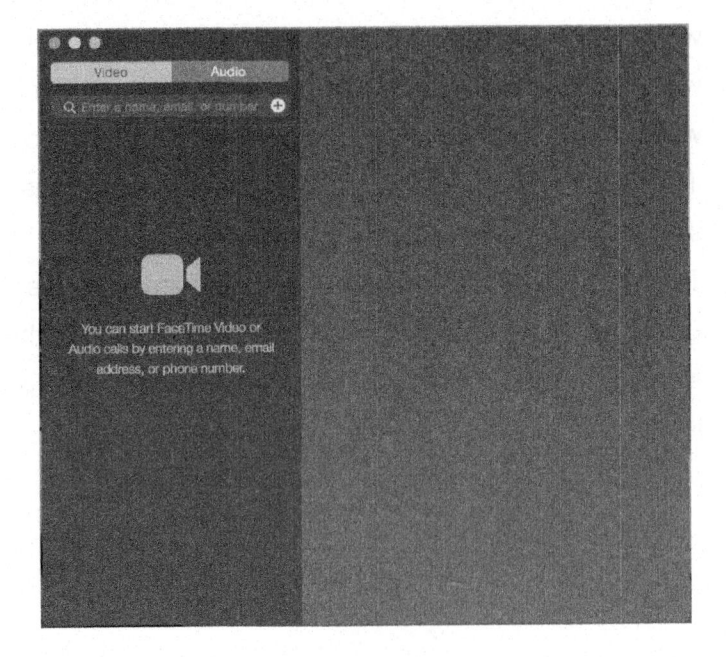

On the left side you can enter a person's name if they are in your Contacts, or a phone number. For FaceTime to work, the other person must also have an Apple device, and accept your call. If you prefer to talk to someone without showing off your dashing good looks, you can switch to audio-only by clicking the Audio tab.

iTunes

If you've used an iPod or iPhone, chances are you've probably installed iTunes on your computer whether it was a Mac or Windows PC. iTunes is the portal where you can manage your Apple devices, browse the iTunes store where you can purchase and download songs, podcasts, TV shows and movies, and import your music collection so it will stay organized and sync harmoniously across all of your Apple devices.

There are five tabs to switch between: My Music, Playlists, Match, Radio, and iTunes Store. At the very left of the window you will see small icons depicting a music note, movie film, TV, and an ellipses. Here you'll be able to switch between what type of media you would like to browse through. For this guide we will be going over the music portion since the other sections are very similar, only smaller.

My Music

In My Music, you'll be able to browse through your personal music collection and play any songs you're hankering for. At the far right there will be a small dropdown labeled Albums by default. Click it to open up the sorting menu to help you better find what you're looking for. You can browse by song, album, artist, composers if you're fancy, and genres. You can also filter old songs so you can view only the latest additions.

Adding Music to your Library

This section is for adding music you already own and have on the computer. If you don't have any music, you should probably skip ahead to the iTunes Store section first.

1. At the top menu bar, click File > Add to Library.
2. When the window comes up, use the left bars to search for the specific song or songs that you'd like to add.
3. If you already have a giant music collection that you may have carried over from an old computer, you can import entire folders at once.
4. When you've decided what to add, click on it once to highlight it, and select the blue Open button.
5. It may take some time depending on how many songs you are importing, but iTunes will show you the progress.
6. Once complete, click on the My Music tab again to verify that your music has been added to the iTunes collection.

Playlists

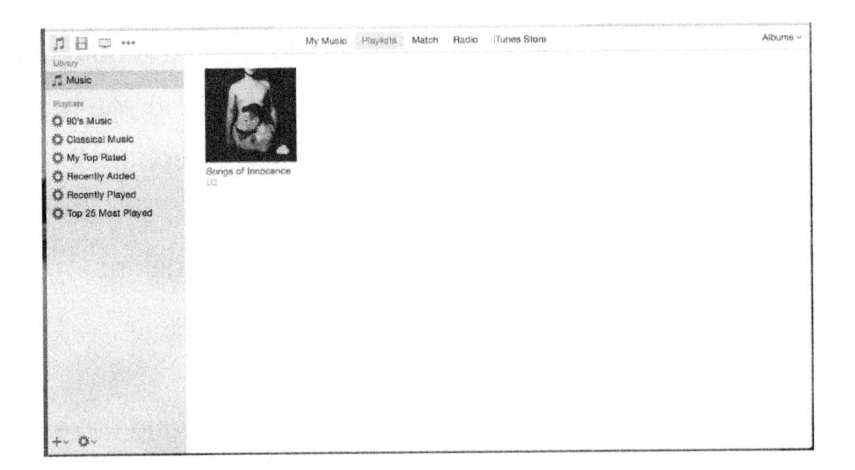

The Playlists section is where you can view, edit and delete playlists you may have created. On the left hand side you will notice that Apple has created some for you: 90's Music, Classical Music, My Top Rated, Recently Added, Recently Played, and Top 25 Most Played. These are pretty self-explanatory, and Apple uses a song's built-in metadata to determine which songs will fit in those premade playlists.

At the top of the list you will also see one called Genius. Selecting Genius will allow you to use Apple's specially made music mixer. It takes songs from your music collection and creates great-sounding custom playlists and mixes.

Using Genius

If this is the first time you are using Genius, you will have to first click on the button that says Turn On Genius.

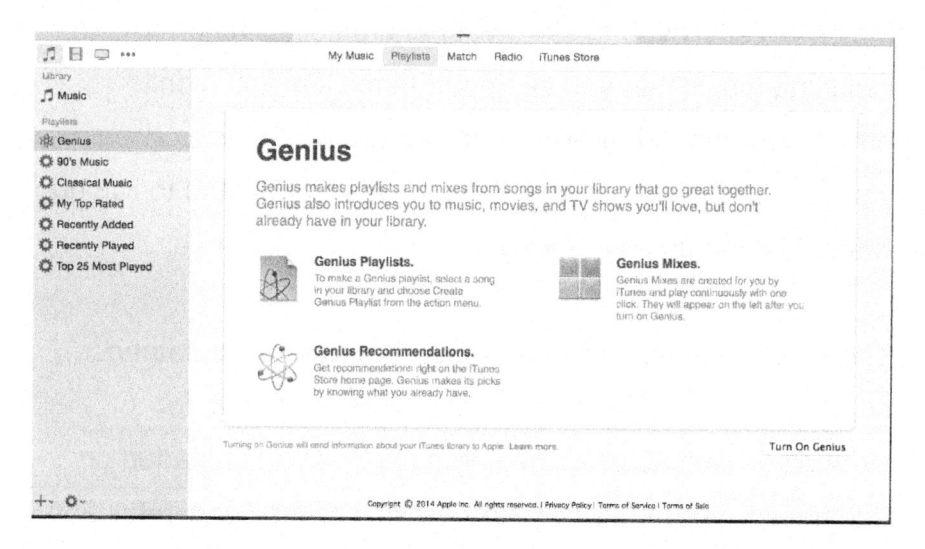

Once you turn it on, there will be three steps that happen automatically. Depending on the size of your library, this may take a while so grab a snack. Once it's finished, your computer screen will greet you with a message that says Genius has been successfully turned on.

That's really all there is to it. Now when you want to create a Genius playlist, just find a song that fits the mood you're looking for, highlight and right click (control + click), and select Create Genius Playlist.

Match

iTunes Match is great if you have a large music library but don't have enough storage on your phone. Signing up for Match will allow you to store your entire collection on iCloud, including music that you've ripped from CDs and didn't purchase through iTunes. This way you'll be able to stream your entire library from any Apple device connected to iCloud without taking up any storage.

The songs are "matched" by Apple's online music database, so when you are playing the song on your iPhone, for example, it isn't actually the same file that you uploaded or purchased. Rather, it's Apple's version of the song in full 256 Kbps, even if the song you originally uploaded or purchased was of lower audio quality. If the song is not found on Apple's own servers (your cousin's Whitesnake cover band perhaps), it will playback the original file you uploaded, with the original audio quality.

Unfortunately, iTunes Match isn't free. If you'd like to sign up for it, expect to pay $24.99 for a yearly subscription. Signing up for Match does have another perk though – if you enjoy using iTunes Radio but can't stand the ads, purchasing the yearly Match subscription will remove ads from Radio.

Radio

Speaking of Radio, that's the fourth tab in iTunes. Radio is a free music streaming service by the music-lovers at Apple. Based on several different factors, Apple creates radio stations that you will probably enjoy. As you listen to different things, the stations will become more and more personalized, playing songs that are more in line with what you've been recently listening to and avoiding the ones you haven't played.

If you would like to explore the radio a little more, you can browse through artist-curated playlists created with a specific goal in mind, or just search by genre. You may also find First Plays, which allows you to listen to entire albums before buying them. This feature only works on select albums, however, so don't expect to find every album available for First Play.

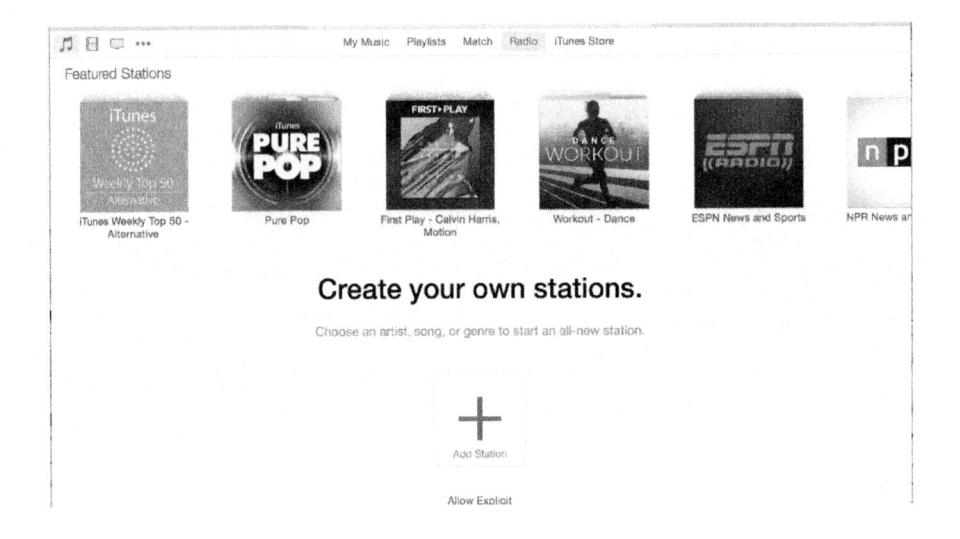

Creating a Radio Station

1. To play a new radio station, open up iTunes and click on the Radio tab.
2. If this is the first time you've used Radio, you will have to click on the blue button that says Start Listening.
3. When Radio fully loads, you will notice that the top half of the window is filled with premade radio stations like Smooth Jazz, Classic Rock, iTunes Weekly Top 50 Dance, or Pepsi

Pulse Pop if you like listening to bubbly pop backed by a giant soda company. Clicking on one will automatically start playing that radio station. At the bottom of the screen you can also toggle explicit language on or off.
4. If these stations just aren't cutting it, you can create your own by clicking the gigantic + button that says Add Station.
5. You can choose a genre as a starting point; or, if you'd like to be more specific, use the search bar to enter the name of an artist, song, or genre that you'd like to listen to. The results will be similar music to what you originally searched for.
6. The station will begin playing and you can see the track information at the top of iTunes, but the main different with Radio is that since you don't already own the music, you'll be able to see how much it'd cost to buy the song currently playing.

iTunes Store

If you don't own any music yet and are looking to start building a digital song collection, or if you own music but would like to add new tracks, the iTunes store is where you can browse, purchase and download new music. In addition to music you can also buy movies, TV shows, podcasts, audiobooks, and books.

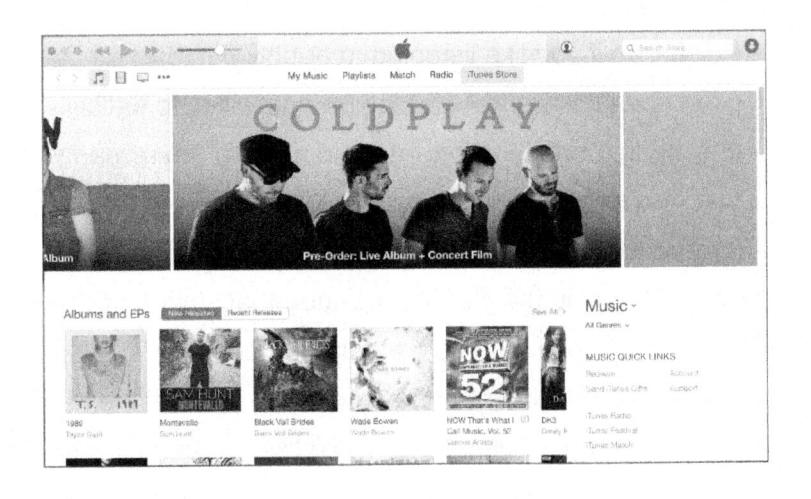

Clicking on the search bar in the top right-hand corner will pull up trending searches in case you are looking for what's hot. If you are looking for a specific song or movie, type it into the search bar and iTunes will load it for you. Scroll through the main page and the latest releases will be shown front and center, letting you see new music at a glance.

On the right side of the screen you will see Music in big letters, with All Genres under it. Clicking the All Genres link opens a dropdown menu with every main genre you can think of.

The big Music link will open a dropdown with the rest of the iTunes store options: Movies, TV shows, App Store, Books, Podcasts, Audiobooks, and iTunes U. Go through each one and you will see that they all follow the same conventions as the Music page, with charts, top downloads, and new releases.

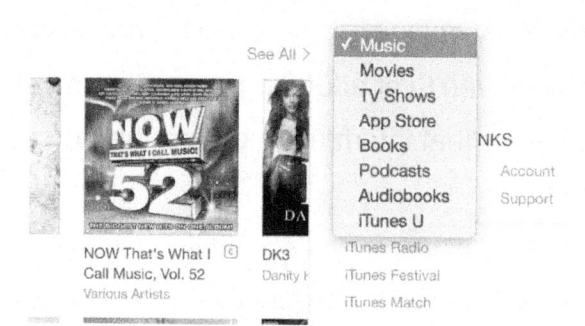

To purchase new music (or any other media) that interests you, use either the search bar or browse through the categories to find what you're looking for. When you reach a song or album you'd like, click it to bring up the full information menu for that item.

The window will display all types of information including album price, individual song price, track list, audio previews, release date, ratings, reviews, and similar items. To buy the album (or a single song), click on the price. A prompt window will come up to make sure you really wanted to buy that album, and you can continue by clicking the blue Buy button.

If you already have funds in your iTunes account, or have a card on file, the purchase will be made and the song(s) will begin to automatically download. If you don't have any money in the account, or haven't yet added a payment method, you will be asked to enter that information before the purchase can be made.

After your purchases are fully downloaded, you'll be able to enjoy your new music by clicking on the My Music tab and selecting your latest addition.

App Store

The App Store is where you'll be able to download and install many different applications that have been developed specifically for use with a Mac computer. These apps will do everything from add new functionalities and make your life easier, to providing a fun way to waste time and play some games during downtime at work. Keep in mind that for the App Store to be functional, you need to be connected to the Internet.

Open the App Store by selecting it either through the dock or Launchpad. The App Store's home page will greet you, showing you the latest and greatest in the world of apps.

At the top you will see different sections: Featured, Top Charts, Categories, Purchases, and Updates.

The Featured, Top Charts, and Categories tabs will show you apps that can be downloaded, but organized in different ways. Featured will show you Best New Apps, Best New Games, Editor's Choices, and collections of different apps that work great together.

Top Charts shows you the best of the best when it comes to available apps, and is broken down by Top Paid, Top Free, and Top Grossing. On the right side, you can also browse through Top Apps broken down by category, in case you wanted to refine your search.

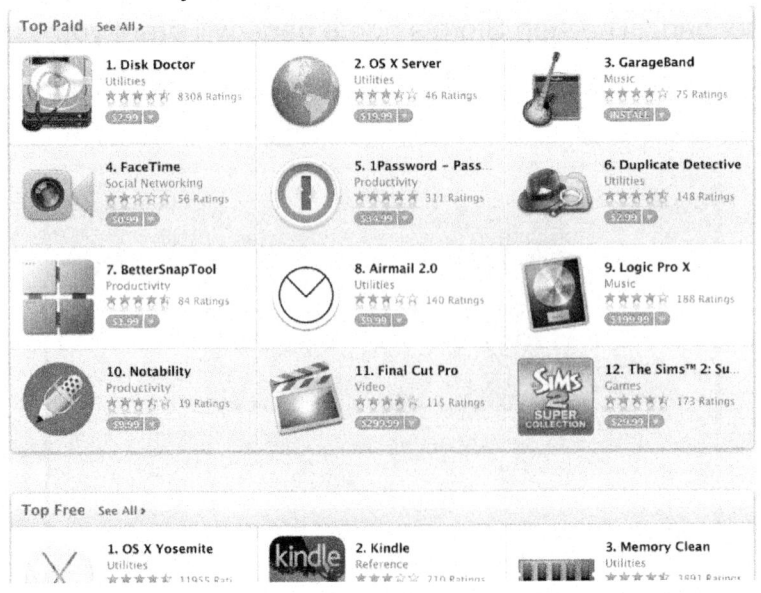

Categories further breaks down your app hunting into different categories like Business, Education, Reference, Productivity, Medical, Entertainment, and Games.

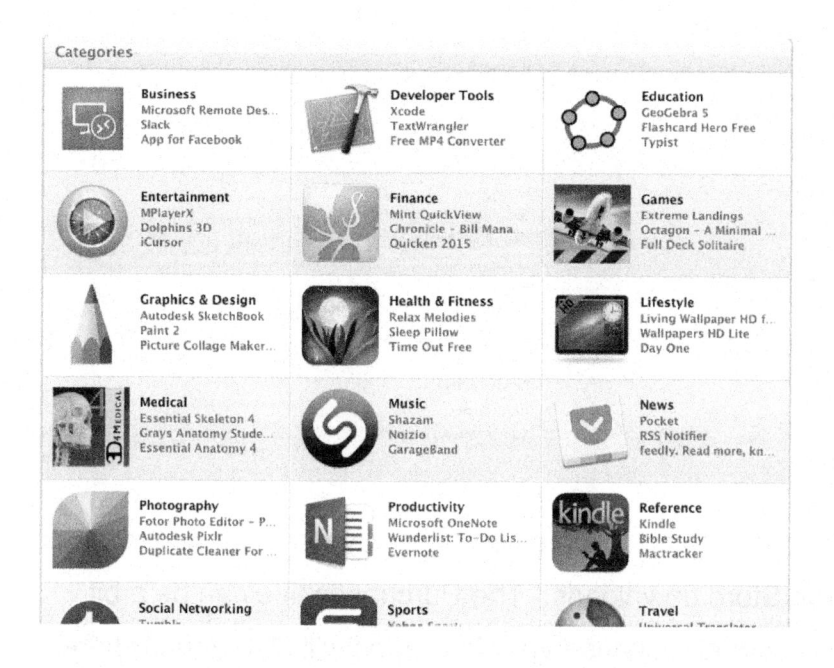

Choosing a category will bring up more selections, and the right side will be filled with even more categories. For example, selecting the Business category will bring you to the main Business apps page where the hottest apps are listed. On the right side, smaller categories like Apps for Writers, App Development, or Apps for Designers can be selected. It doesn't matter what category of apps you are currently under; the list remains the same in the right half.

Top Charts Categories
All Categories
Business
Developer Tools
Education
Entertainment
Finance
Games
Graphics & Design
Health & Fitness
Lifestyle
Medical
Music
News
Photography
Productivity
Reference
Social Networking

Purchases and Updates are where you can go to view past App Store downloads. The Purchases title can be a bit misleading, because your free apps will also appear here. In the Updates section, you can view which apps need to be updated to the latest version. If you have multiple apps that need updating, you can choose the Update All button and it will go down the entire list.

Customizing Your Mac

A great deal of settings on your Mac can be changed to better suit your needs. Everything from the obvious stuff like changing your wallpaper to the little things like how sensitive the mouse pointer is. All of the settings and customization options occur through System Preferences. If you were a Windows user, System Preferences is like the Control Panel for Mac. In this section, we will explore System Preferences and check out some of the great things you can do here.

There are a number of ways to open System Preferences:

- On your dock or using the Launchpad, you will find the System Preferences icon that looks like a grey square icon with a gear inside of it.

- On the top menu bar, you can click on the Apple icon and one of the dropdown options will be System Preferences.

- You can also jump to different sections of System Preferences by pressing the Option key along with a button at the top of your keyboard. For example, pressing Option + F5 (keyboard brightness) will take you right to the keyboard settings. Pressing Option + F3 (Mission Control) will take you to the Mission Control settings.

- You can also press Command (⌘) + Space bar to run Spotlight search, type in the setting you'd like to jump to (Displays or iCloud for example), and hit return.

General

Click on the General tab to access many different options that don't necessarily fall under any other category. Here is an overview of what some of the options are:

- You can change the appearance of the main buttons, windows, and menus by selecting either Blue or Graphite.

- The highlight color can also be changed between various colors.

- New to OS X Yosemite, you can change the top menu bar and dock to dark colors. This option works great with dark wallpapers.

- Scroll bars can be set to display automatically based on mouse or trackpad, only when scrolling, or always on.

- The default web browser can also be selected here.

- Here is where you can allow Handoff to work between your Mac and iCloud devices.

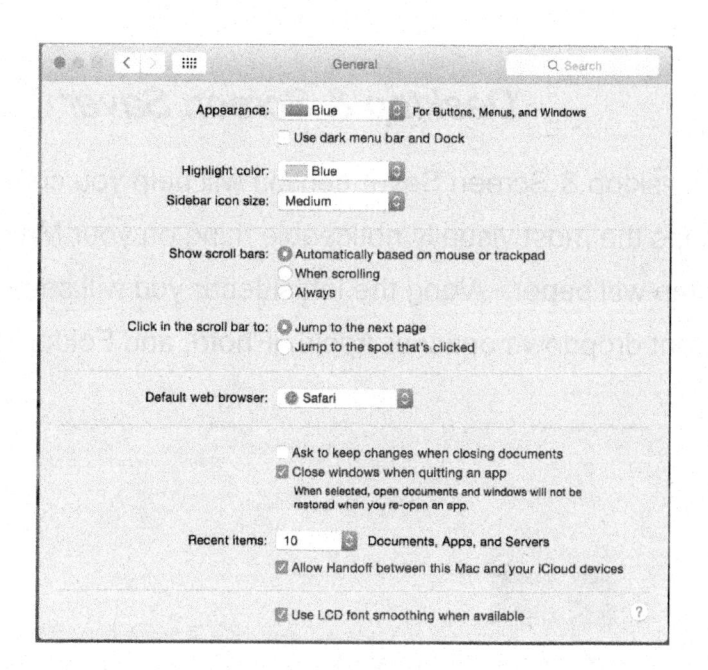

Appearance:	Blue	For Buttons, Menus, and Windows
	☐ Use dark menu bar and Dock	
Highlight color:	Blue	
Sidebar icon size:	Medium	
Show scroll bars:	● Automatically based on mouse or trackpad ○ When scrolling ○ Always	
Click in the scroll bar to:	● Jump to the next page ○ Jump to the spot that's clicked	
Default web browser:	Safari	

☐ Ask to keep changes when closing documents
☑ Close windows when quitting an app
   When selected, open documents and windows will not be restored when you re-open an app.

Recent items: 10   Documents, Apps, and Servers

☑ Allow Handoff between this Mac and your iCloud devices

☑ Use LCD font smoothing when available

Desktop & Screen Saver

The Desktop & Screen Saver section will help you change perhaps the most visually noticeable thing on your Mac – the desktop wallpaper. Along the left sidebar you will see several different dropdown options: Apple, iPhoto, and Folders .

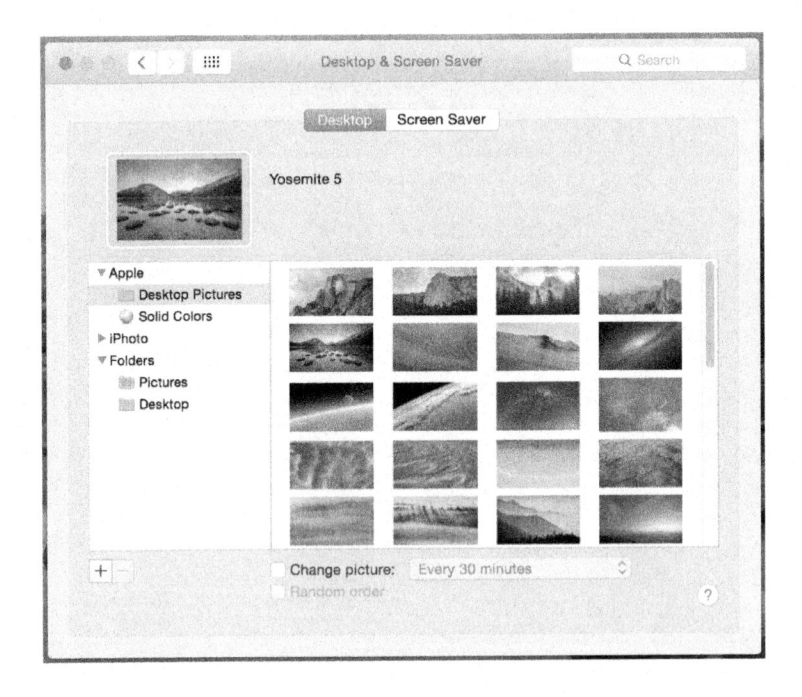

At the bottom, you will be able to change the picture every so often, and you can choose how often you'd like a new image to refresh. The images that show up in the right-hand window will be the ones that get scrolled through during refreshes.

86

To change your desktop wallpaper to one of the great-looking images provided by Apple, or if you just want to browse the available choices, click on the Apple name. A bunch of colorful, high-resolution images will populate the right-hand side, and you can scroll through the list to find something you like. Clicking on an image will change your wallpaper to that particular selection. If you're a plain Jane and prefer to keep things really simple, you can also select Solid Colors to find an array of potentially yawn-inducing plain wallpapers.

Selecting iPhoto will let you scroll through your photos, allowing you to select a cherished memory as your wallpaper.

The Folders option will let you choose between added folders where more image files might be lying in wait. If you save lots of images to your desktop, you might want to add the Desktop folder here so you can include those images as would-be wallpapers.

Adding and Removing Folders
1. To add new folders and image collections, click on the + button located at the bottom of the left sidebar.
2. When the window comes up, search for the folder that you'd like to add.
3. Once you find the desired folder, click the blue Choose button to confirm the changes.

4. To remove a folder, highlight the folder that you'd like deleted and then click the – button to remove it.

Screen Saver

The screen saver. A great opportunity to show the world (or the library you're sitting in) your favorite family photos, dream getaways, or fancy art. Or just silly cat pictures. Either way, screen savers are fun. To set one up, click on the Screen Saver button at the top of the Desktop & Screen Saver window.

The left sidebar will have more options than you probably need when it comes to different ways to display your pictures. Some great ones you will probably like are Shuffling Tiles, Vintage Prints, and Classic.

On the right side you can see a preview of what your screen saver will look like. In this part of the window you can also select a source: National Geographic, Aerial, Cosmos, Nature Patterns, and Choose Folder if you have a particular folder of images you'd like to use. If you'd like to shuffle the order in which images appear, check the box next to Shuffle slide order.

At the very bottom of the window you can choose the length of time before the screen saver starts. You'll also be able to pick if you'd like to display the clock or not.

Mission Control

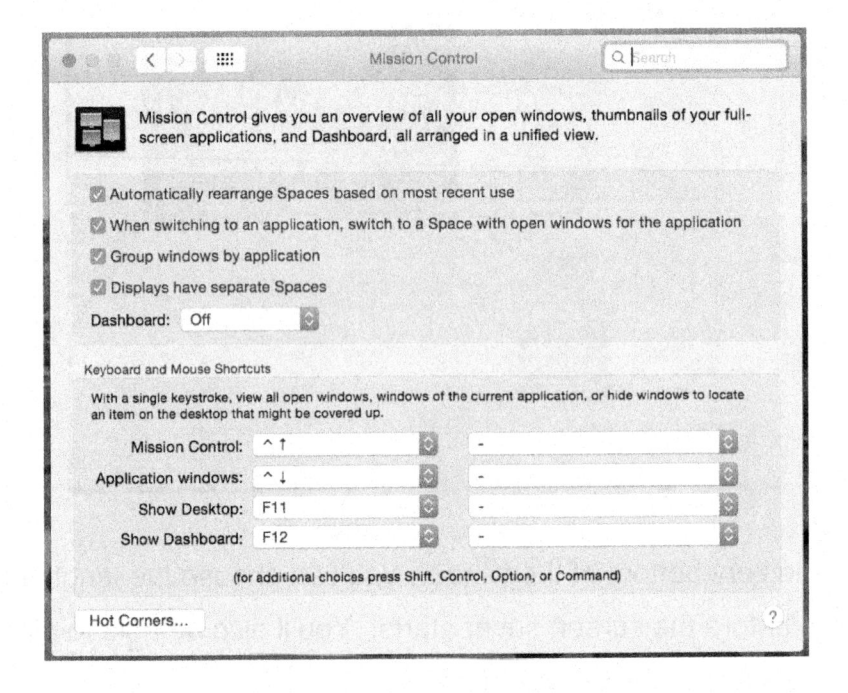

Mission Control is where you can control, you guessed it, settings related to Mission Control! Checking the top four checkboxes can be a good idea if you want to keep your workspace neat and organized. You can also choose to have the Dashboard window off, as an overlay, or as Space (a separate window you can switch to). The bottom half of the section will allow you to change the keyboard shortcuts for Mission Control, Application windows, and viewing the desktop or dashboard.

Dock

The dock, as mentioned early on, is the area where shortcuts to frequently used files and applications can be stored. Under dock settings, you will see two sliders at the top of the window: Size, and Magnification. The Size slider will determine how large your dock appears, and Magnification (if checked on) will give you that cool magnifying effect when you hover over an icon in the dock. Sliding left or right will make the magnification effect smaller or larger respectively.

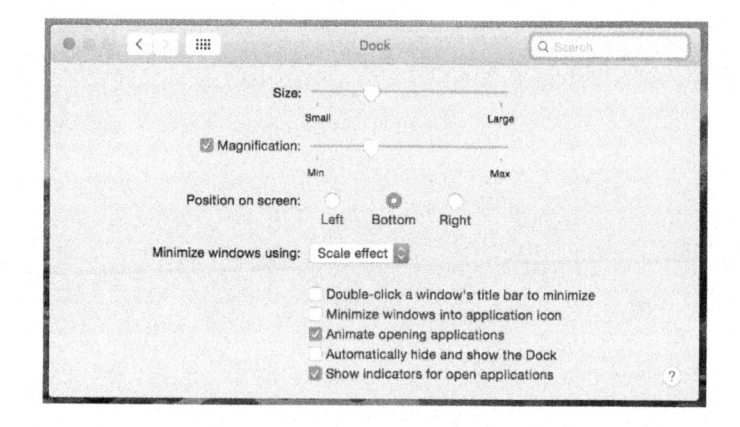

The bottom half of the window will have a few other options. You can choose the position of the dock, by selecting the radio button for Left, Bottom, or Right. By default, the dock is positioned at the bottom. The following option will give you the option to change the effect a minimized window has; you can choose either a genie effect to see the window whimsically slide down as if the dock were a genie bottle, or scale effect to see the window shrink as it makes its way down.

Sound

The Sound menu is where all changes related to sound effects and sound in general can be modified. There are three tabs that you can switch between.

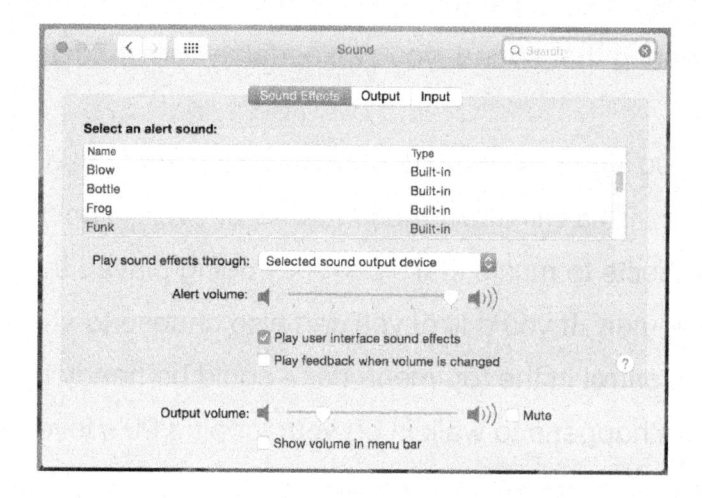

Sound Effects

The Sound Effects tab is where you can select an alert sound from the many different built-in options. By default, the following dropdown menu should be set to Selected sound output device to play the chosen sound effects through your standard speakers.

The next two checkboxes let you turn sound effects on or off for the user interface, and for volume control. If you are coming from an older version of OS X, you will notice that the annoying but beloved "bweek bweek" sound effect is gone when you press the volume up or volume down keys. With OS X Yosemite, the sound effect is defaulted to off, but if you miss hearing that sound, you can certainly turn it back on.

Lastly, you'll be able to adjust the output volume of your speakers. This will affect the loudness of everything from sound effects to music that's currently being played through the computer. If you'd like, you can also choose to show the volume control in the top menu bar – could be handy if someone happens to walk in on your looping 90's love ballads playlist.

Input & Output

The input and output tabs are both very similar. Each will let you change the device for sound input or output (speakers or microphones), as well as adjust sound settings. In the Output tab, you can adjust the slider to move the balance left or right, and in Input, you can change the microphone's input volume and enable or disable the built-in noise reduction feature in case you frequently use your Mac's microphone in busy cafes or while cruising on the freeway in your shiny red convertible (please don't do that).

Users & Groups

If there is going to be more than one person using the Mac, you will probably want to set up different users and groups to keep things organized. Open up the Users & Groups window by going to System Preferences > Users & Groups.

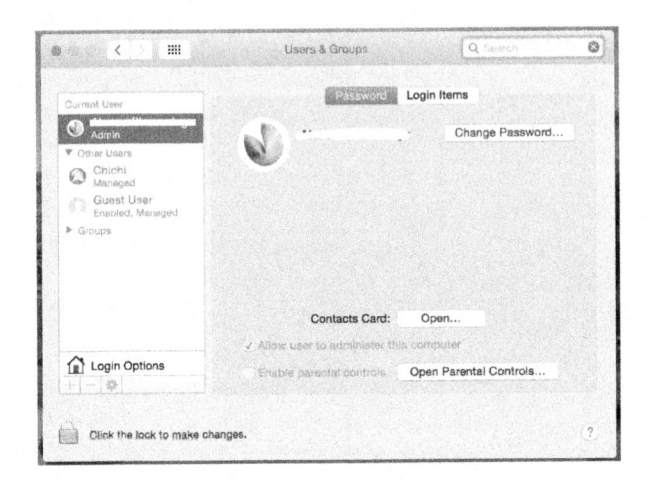

Along the left sidebar all existing users and groups (if you have any) will be laid out for you. Feel free to click around each one and explore the options that are made available. In order to make any changes, click on the lock icon at the lower left corner so that it looks unlocked. You will also be prompted to enter your administrator password before continuing.

- Selecting the Admin user account will let you change the login password, open up the Contacts card and enable parental controls. Clicking the Login Items will allow you to change the applications that start running automatically each time you log in.

- Any other created users will give you the options to enable parental controls, change password, or turn that account into another administrator account that has full control of the Mac.

- By default you will see a Guest user set up. If it's selected, you can choose to disable the Guest user from being available as a login option. You can also set parental controls and allow guest access to your shared folders. If you do choose to keep the Guest user, keep in mind that there will be no password required, and all information and files created during that session will be deleted upon logging out.

- At the bottom of the left sidebar there is another option, called Login Options. Here you'll find different options such as automatic login, show password hints, and show the Sleep, Shut Down, and Restart buttons. You can also display your full name or user name at the top right of the menu bar by checking the box next to Show fast user switching menu and making a selection.

Create New Users

If you'd prefer to keep your business separated from the peeping eyes of others who might share the computer, creating new users is a great idea. Managing existing users is easy once you set them up.

1. To create a new user, click on the + button.

2. From the New dropdown menu, choose from the following options: Administrator, Standard, Managed with Parental Controls, or Sharing Only.

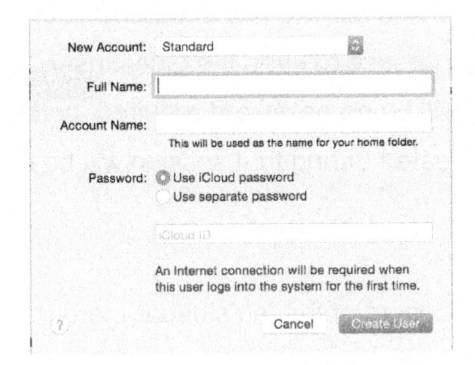

![New Account dialog showing Standard account type with fields for Full Name, Account Name, Password options (Use iCloud password or Use separate password), and iCloud ID. Text reads "This will be used as the name for your home folder." and "An Internet connection will be required when this user logs into the system for the first time." with Cancel and Create User buttons.]

3. Fill in the Full Name and Account Name fields.

4. You can choose to have the new user log in using an existing iCloud account and password, or create a whole new password.

5. If you selected Use iCloud Password, you will be prompted to enter the associated iCloud ID.

6. If you instead chose to opt for a newly created password, you will be asked to enter it twice to verify. It's also recommended that you create some sort of hint that will remind the user of the password.

7. Once finished, click the blue Create User button. If you chose to use an iCloud ID, you will be asked to enter the password. If you made a new password, you don't need to do anything else.

Removing Existing Users

1. To remove currently existing users, select the user that you'd like to delete.

2. With that user highlighted, click on the – button.

3. A prompt will appear asking if you are really sure you'd like to remove the user from the computer.

4. You can also choose from one of three radio buttons: save the home folder, leave the home folder alone, or delete the home folder.

5. Once you've made a decision, click the blue Delete User button to confirm your choice and make the changes happen.

Creating Groups

If it gets to the point that you have a ton of users and need a better way to managed them while staying organized, it may be a great time to use user groups. Groups can be created to separate all of your kids' accounts, your own, and maybe friends or roommates. By using groups you will be able to assign special file and folder privileges to the entire group of users instead of having to manually set each one's limits.

1. To create a new group, go to System Preferences > Users & Groups.

2. Make sure the lock icon is clicked open, and enter your administrator password when prompted.

3. At the bottom of the left sidebar, click the + button.

4. From the New dropdown menu, select Group

5. In the Full Name field, create and enter a name for your group.

6. Click the blue Create Group button to confirm.

7. The new group will be created, and you will be able to check boxes next to each existing user to designate who will be a part of this group. If you have existing groups, you can also select entire groups to be a part of yet another group.

Setting Permissions

The main purpose of creating groups is to limit permissions and designate privileges to multiple users at the same time.

1. To begin, find a disk, file or folder that you'd like your new group to have certain permissions on.

2. Highlight the item by clicking on it once.

3. Go to File > Get Info or right-click and select Get Info.

4. On the Info window, at the very bottom there should be a section called Sharing & Permissions. Click on the triangle to the left of it to expand.

5. You will see that there are a few permissions already set. To add more users and groups, click on the + button. You may be required to enter your administrator password to continue.

6. Find the users or groups that you'd like to change permissions for, and click the blue Select button.

7. You should see the new user or group added to the list of allowed users, and next to it under the Privileges column their default permissions.

8. Click on the permissions to change it between Read Only, Write Only, or Read & Write.

Parental Controls

The Internet can be a scary place, especially if your kids are starting to use computers. Apple understands what parents are worried about, and they've developed a great built-in tool to help you control the computer use of your children.

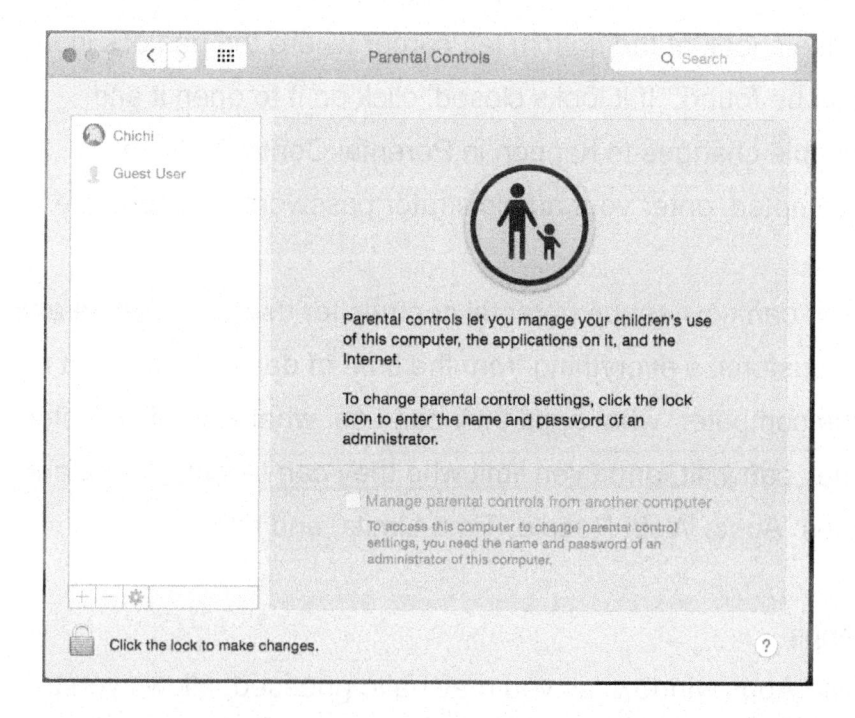

Before continuing, be sure to have a User account created for your child. If you skipped past the previous section (our feelings might be hurt, but don't worry about it), go to System Preferences > Users & Groups, and add a new user. Name it after your child, or maybe a cute nickname you've given them.

Take a look at the bottom left corner where the padlock icon can be found. If it looks closed, click on it to open it and enable changes to happen in Parental Controls. When prompted, enter your administrator password and continue.

You can now set up parental controls for users! You'll be able to customize everything from the time of day or time spent on the computer, what apps they can use, what kind of websites they can visit, and even limit who they can talk to. There are 5 tabs: Apps, Web, People, Time Limits, and Other.

Apps
The Apps window, as you may have guessed, allows you to customize the restrictions on apps and widgets. You can also turn on the Simple Finder by checking the box next to it. Simple Finder is a much simpler version of the Finder on your Mac, and is a great option for younger users, or even those who aren't too familiar with using computers in general.

[Screenshot of Parental Controls Apps window]

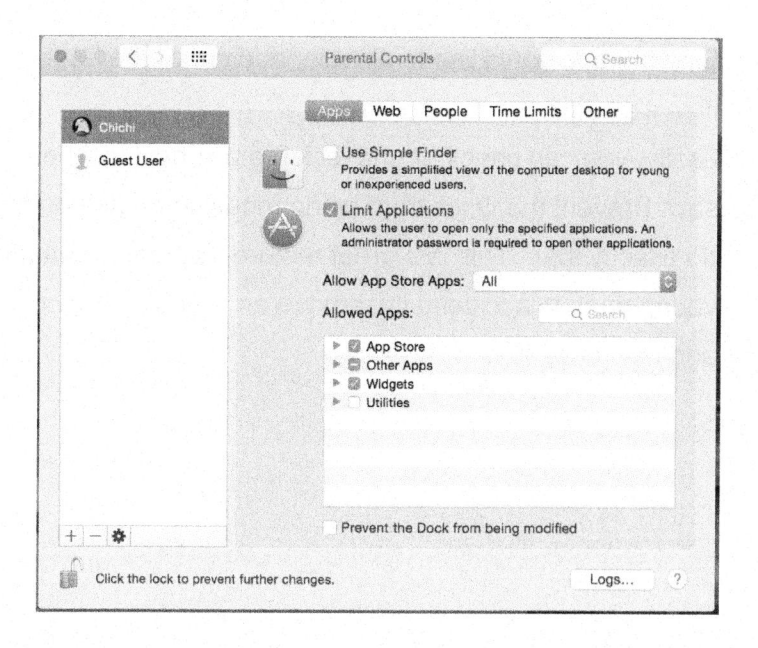

The rest of the Apps window needs to be enabled by checking the box next to Limit Applications. Here's where the good stuff is!

- The dropdown menu labeled Allow App Store Apps will allow you to filter installed programs by age recommendation. For example, if you select up to 12+ selected, any applications that are rated 17+ won't be useable by your little one. You can also select Don't Allow to block all applications from being use, and All to allow all applications to be used.
- The next section, Allowed Apps, lets you refine your blocks to individual applications. If you have up to 12+ installed but there are a few programs you don't want the kids to use that fall under that age category, you can click on the dropdown arrow next to App Store, Other Apps, Widgets, or Utilities.

Find the app you'd like to disable, and check the box next to it so it's blank.
- Lastly, you can check or uncheck the box next to where it says Prevent the Dock from being modified at the bottom, to do exactly that. This is a great feature if you don't want your young ones to accidentally remove an app from the dock or add new ones to it.

Web

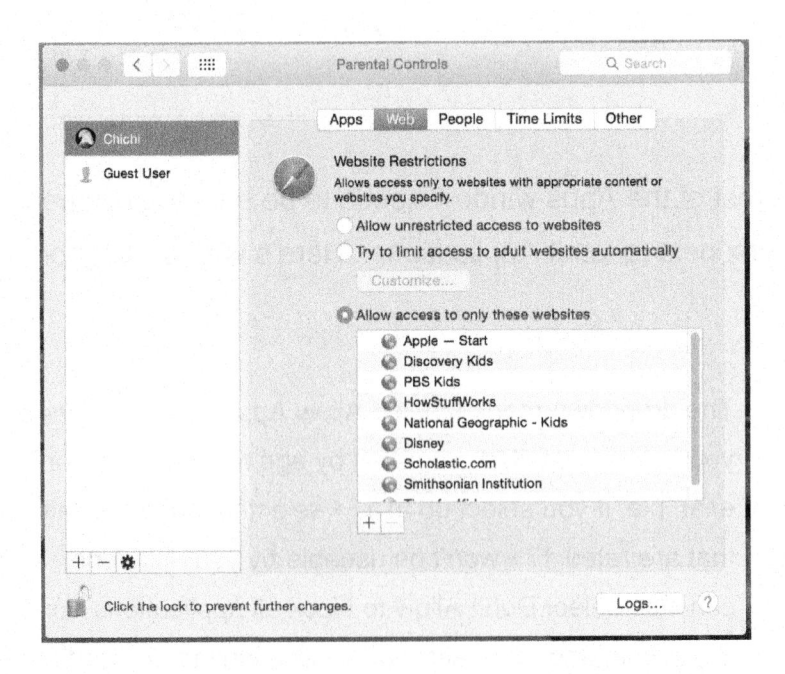

The Web tab is where you can rule the Internet with an iron fist, at least in the eyes of your kids.

- There are two radio buttons at the top of the window: Allow unrestricted access to websites (not such a good idea with younger children), and Try to limit access to adult websites automatically. If you know of any particular websites that might not seem adult at first, or just want to explicitly deny certain ogling sites, you can click the Customize button and create a list of sites that you will always allow them to visit, or always block.

- Better yet, you can click on the third radio button that says Allow access to only these websites. Selecting this button will limit your child's Internet usage to only the websites listed. Feel free to use the + and − buttons at the bottom of the window to add or remove sites on the list to your liking.

People

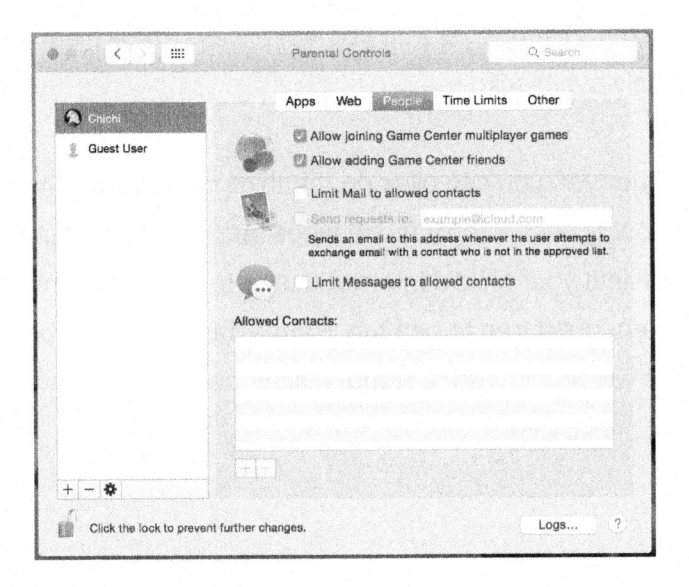

Does your little one use the computer to play games, send emails, or use Messages to instant message friends from school? If you are looking to set up parental controls around these activities, the People tab is how you do it.

- The first two checkboxes at the top of the window are for Game Center, the hub where you can play games, track scores, and keep in touch with other players or hold multiplayer sessions. If you don't want your kids to play multiplayer games, uncheck the box next to Allow joining Game Center multiplayer games. The second box can be checked or unchecked to allow or restrict them from adding friends on Game Center.

- After the Game Center options, you can limit Messages or Mail to allowed contacts only. If your child tries to send an email to someone that is not on the Allowed Contacts list, you can check the Send requests box and enter your email address to receive an alert.

- At the bottom, as with the Web tab, you will be able to add or remove people from the Allowed Contacts list by using the + or – buttons.

Time Limits

Limiting the amount of time the kids spend on the computer can be a good idea, especially if they have plenty of homework throughout the week and you'd like them to get some fresh air and play outside more often. The Time Limits tab can help with that!

- The top part of the window is devoted to weekday (Monday through Friday) and weekend (Saturday and Sunday) time limits. The default values (when the appropriate boxes are checked) are a maximum time of 3 hours spent on the computer during the week, and 5 hours on the weekend. If you'd like to change it, just drag the slider. The time ranges between a minimum of 30 minutes and a maximum of 8 hours.

- The bottom section, called Bedtime, prevents your children from using the computer during specific windows of time. If they should be in bed by 8pm and wake up around 6am, you can block their computer usage during this time in case they wake up in the middle of the night and wander over to the shiny Mac.

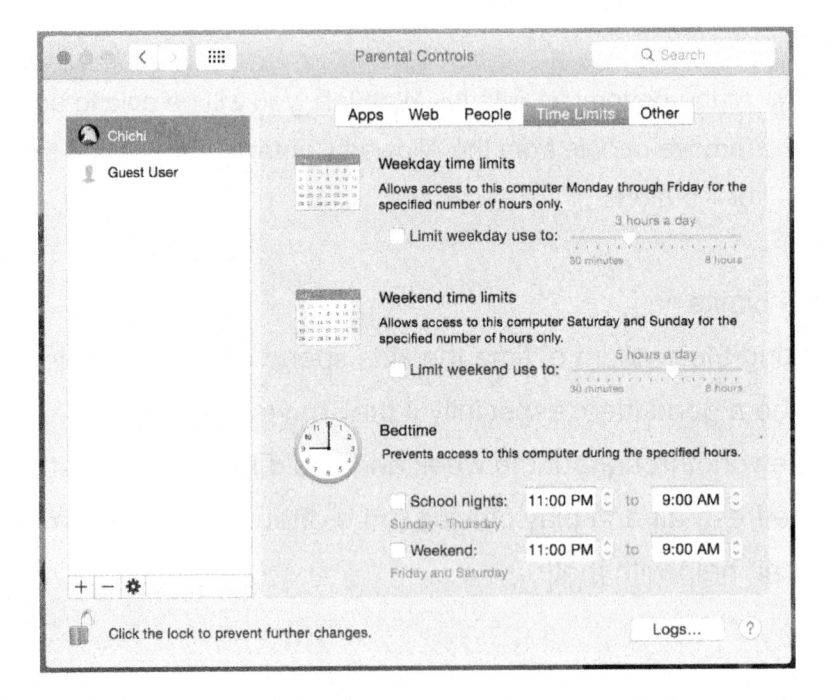

Other

The last tab, Other, is a list of miscellaneous items that you can allow or block. These options include disabling the built-in camera, hiding profanity in Dictionary, the ability to change their password, and printer administration to prevent your little ones from adding your work printer to the network and printing out full-page black squares.

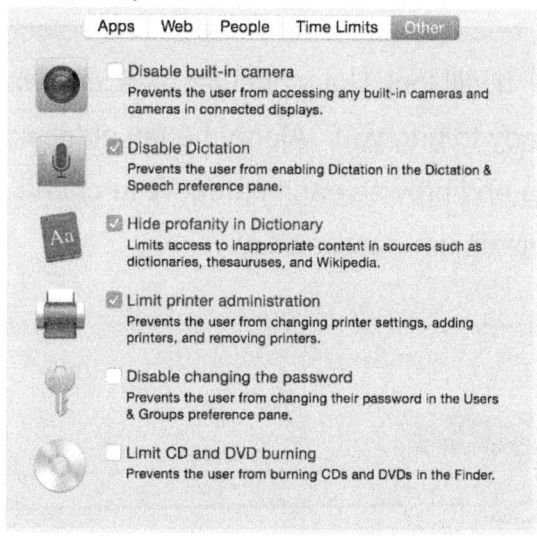

| Apps | Web | People | Time Limits | Other |

- Disable built-in camera
  Prevents the user from accessing any built-in cameras and cameras in connected displays.

- ☑ Disable Dictation
  Prevents the user from enabling Dictation in the Dictation & Speech preference pane.

- ☑ Hide profanity in Dictionary
  Limits access to inappropriate content in sources such as dictionaries, thesauruses, and Wikipedia.

- ☑ Limit printer administration
  Prevents the user from changing printer settings, adding printers, and removing printers.

- Disable changing the password
  Prevents the user from changing their password in the Users & Groups preference pane.

- Limit CD and DVD burning
  Prevents the user from burning CDs and DVDs in the Finder.

Accessibility

As with the iPhones and iPads, Apple has taken great care to make sure as many people can use their products as possible, with or without disabilities. This is reflected by how many options are available under the Accessibility menu. To access Accessibility, open System Preferences and select Accessibility. It will look like a circular blue icon with a guy that looks ready to hug you. Along the left sidebar, you can scroll through and browse each category to change or adjust settings for maximum accessibility.

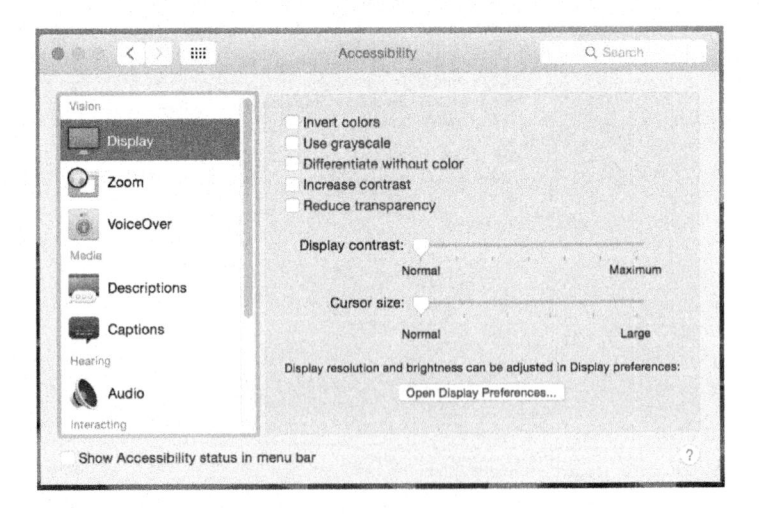

Vision

The Display tab will show you many different settings you can change to make the screen easier to look at. There are all kinds of vision impairments, and Apple hopes to target each one: you can choose to invert colors, use grayscale, differentiate without color, increase contrast, and reduce transparency. Additionally, you can also adjust the sliders for display contrast and cursor size.

Zoom allows you to create a zoomed in effect on a small area of the screen by using keyboard shortcuts. There are different keys that can be assigned to zoom in or out, smooth images, and whether you want to zoom into the entire screen or just a specific section.

If you have visual disabilities and own an iPhone or iPad, you may already be using VoiceOver, that extremely useful feature that provides spoken descriptions of everything you click, highlight, or scroll through. To enable VoiceOver, click the checkbox next to it. You will be able to toggle VoiceOver on or off by pressing Command (⌘)+ F5.

Media

The Media section includes a few different settings for audio and video playback. Click on Descriptions to enable spoken descriptions for videos. There is only one option here to turn video descriptions on or off.

Captions will apply subtitles and captions to videos. You can select from Default, Classic (if you want to feel like you're in the 80's again), or Large Text. If you aren't happy with any of these choices and would prefer to make your own, the ball is in your court. Click on the + or – buttons to add or remove caption settings. If you click the + button, you will be able to choose font type, color, size, and background color. At the bottom you can also choose if you'd prefer closed captions and subtitles for the deaf and hard of hearing (SDH) whenever possible.

Hearing

The Sound tab provides options for hearing disabilities. You can choose to set up a visual flash of the screen each time an alert sound is played, and also decide if you'd like to play stereo audio as mono instead.

Interacting

Keyboard includes settings for Sticky Keys and Slow Keys. Sticky Keys allows certain buttons to remain activated without you having to hold down the key. For example, if you have Sticky Keys turned on and want to copy some text, instead of holding down Command + C at the same time, you could press the Command button first, followed by the C key. When enabled, you'll hear a lock sound, and anytime you use a modifier key like Command, a large icon will appear in the top right corner of the screen indicating that a Sticky Key combination has been started. Slow Keys increases the amount of time between a button press and activation, so if you press Enter, it will take a little longer to actually process.

Mouse & Trackpad features settings like Mouse Keys, which lets you move the mouse around using the number pad on your keyboard, double-click speed, and the option to ignore the built-in trackpad (on MacBooks) if there is a separate mouse or trackpad connected to the computer.

Switch Control requires you to enter your administrator before making any changes, because it's a powerful function that allows you to control the computer using one or more switches that you designate. You can also modify other settings like what to do while navigating, determine pointer precision, and change the size for the Switch Control cursor.

The Dictation tab does exactly what it sounds like – let's you dictate commands and write or edit text using only your voice. To enable dictation, you will first need to click on the bottom button that says Open Dictation & Speech Preferences and selecting the On radio button.

Privacy and Security

If you are using your computer to store pictures, videos, or account information that you don't want anyone else to access, then privacy could be a serious concern you might have thought about. While information may seem safe because you are using a Mac and don't plan on taking it outside of the house (unless it's a MacBook), any connection to the internet could leave you vulnerable.

Creating Strong Passwords

Strong passwords are the first line of defense against potential thieves and criminals looking to grab your stuff. If you create and maintain complex passwords for your most sensitive information, you'll greatly reduce the chances of someone cracking them.

Like the iOS devices, your Mac comes with Keychain Access. By default, Keychain Access has a master password that is identical to whatever you chose as your computer's administrator password. In Keychain Assistant, you can store and keep track of all the accounts and passwords you create. If you are creating a new account and need help making a suitable password, you can also use the built-in Password Assistant.

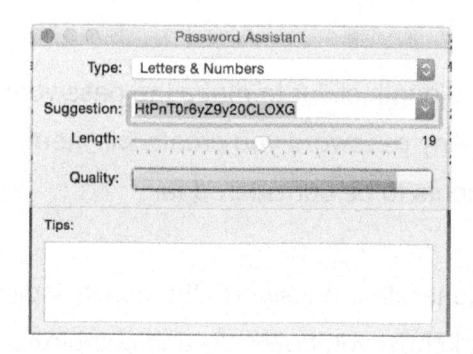

Using Password Assistant

1. First, open up Keychain Access by going to Launchpad > Other > Keychain Access.

2. When it loads, you will be able to view the entire list of accounts that are already synced to Keychain. If you would like to change the password for an account that already exists, find the account and double click on it. If not, click on the + button at the bottom to add a new account.

3. When the new window comes up, take a look at the bottom. There will be a field for password, and at the right of it will be a small key icon. Click the key icon to open up Password Assistant.

4. From Type you can select Manual (create your own), Memorable, Letters & Numbers, Numbers Only, Random, and FIPS-181 compliant.

5. Suggestions will automatically populate, and you can scroll through several different suggestions by using the dropdown menu.

6. Adjust the length slider to make the password longer or shorter. Any password you create will meet at least the requirements to be considered fair.

7. As you generate a password, the quality indicator will change to show you how safe and complex a given password is.

That's it! Since your account is stored in Keychain Access, you don't have to worry about memorizing these crazy big passwords. If you need to reenter them for some reason, you can always come back to the account in Keychain Access and copy and paste the password.

Firewall

Another line of defense you can add is a Firewall, which protects you from unwanted connections to potentially malicious software applications, websites, or files.

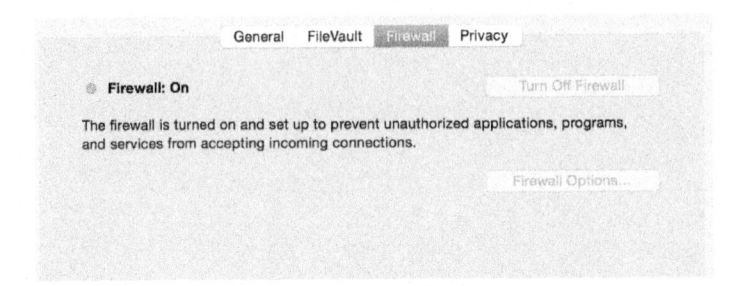

To enable the firewall that comes with your Mac, go to System Preferences > Security & Privacy and select the Firewall tab. Before you can make any changes, click on the lock icon in the bottom left corner and enter your administrator password to continue. You will then be able to turn on the firewall, and open up firewall options. If you'd like to block all incoming connections except for the bare necessities (not related to the Jungle Book song), you can do so by checking off the box at the top.

The most common setting to leave on is the middle one that says Automatically allow signed software to receive incoming connections, which will let applications like Dropbox and Evernote to connect without prompting you each time. The last setting, Stealth Mode, prevents your computer from responding to ping requests by third party software, a useful weapon against hackers who ping computers to find their vulnerable spots.

Find My Mac

In the event that your Mac is lost or stolen, not all is lost. Your Mac comes with a useful feature called Find My Mac that enables you to see where the computer is currently located.

To enable Find My Mac, go to System Preferences > iCloud and check the box next to Find My Mac. Your location services must also be turned on, so go to System Preferences > Security & Privacy > Privacy > Location Services and make sure Enable Location Services is checked on.

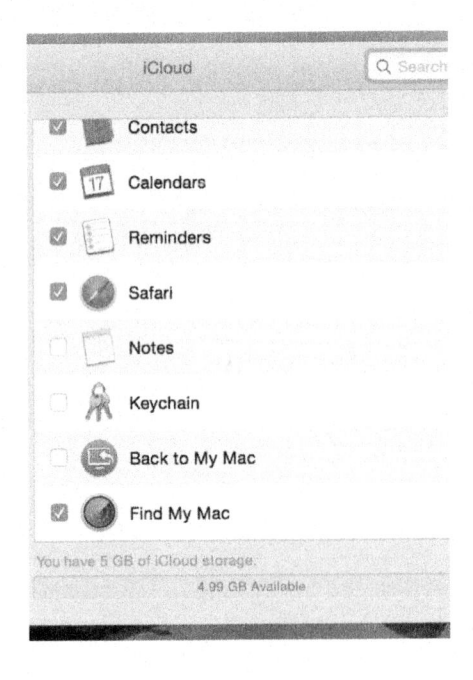

To track your computer, you can log into any computer and visit icloud.com, enter your iCloud login information, and click on Find My Mac. As long as the Mac is awake and connected to the Internet through Wi-Fi or Ethernet, you will be able to play loud sound (great if you might have lost the computer in the couch), lock it, or completely erase it so your private information is removed.

Privacy

Privacy is something Apple feels very strongly about. You can control privacy from the obvious things like your internet browser's settings, down to the more obscure things like which apps can control your accessibility settings, and disabling location settings.

Internet Privacy

Let's start with something you probably use every day. Protecting your privacy online can be difficult with so many websites asking for all kind of information. Safari comes with several different ways to keep things from the prying eyes of the web.

If you'd like to clear your search and browsing history, there are two ways to do it: either by clicking on Safari > Clear History and Website Data or History > Clear History and Website Data. Both can be found on the top menu bar. When the window comes up, you will be able to choose how far back you want the cleansing to reach, and once you make a selection, just press the Clear History button to make the changes final.

Cookies allow websites to store data and track certain things, like what other websites you visit during your Internet session, or what kind of products you tend to look at the most. This information is mostly used by advertisers to better target ads for you, but the option is always there if you'd like to disable them. Open up Safari, and go to Safari > Preferences, then select the Privacy tab. The cookie options range from allowing all websites to store cookies, to blocking all websites. You can also allow cookies only from the most frequently visited websites. If you prefer not to be tracked, check off the box at the bottom that says Ask websites to not track me.

Application Privacy

The other part of privacy is through installed applications. Go to System Preferences > Security & Privacy and click the Privacy tab. You can shut location services off by checking the box next to Enable Location Services. Browse through the left sidebar and you'll be able to customize permissions. If you don't want any apps to access your contacts or calendars, here is where you can block all or some programs from that information.

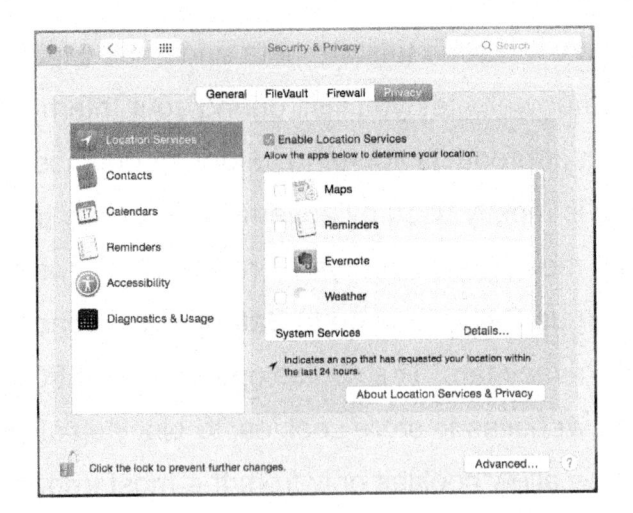

Maintenance

Preserving Battery Life

This section is more for the MacBook users, since desktops don't have internal batteries. If you want to avoid being that person at the café that's forever strapped to the wall with a charger, enjoy your freedom by following these tips to keep your laptop running longer.

- Go to System Preferences > Energy Saver and under the Battery tab, choose to put hard disks to sleep whenever possible, and slightly dim the display while on battery power. Adjust the slider at the top of the window to determine how long your computer should go before shutting off the display. A happy medium would be around 10 or 15 minutes – short enough to kick in if you forgot the computer was on, but long enough that you don't have to worry about the screen shutting off each time you get up and walk away from the computer for a brief moment. Also, while you are here, be sure to check the box at the bottom to show battery percentage as a menulet.

- Keep the screen only as bright as you need to clearly see the screen. This might sound like common sense, but take an airplane ride or two at night and you'll witness several passengers using their MacBooks at maximum brightness even though all lights are off.

- The same goes for the backlit keyboard; go only as bright as you need, and if it's bright enough to see the keys without any help, make sure the backlight illumination is shut off.

- Even though today's computers are made to survive a lot more abuse, it's still a good idea to restart or fully shut down your computer every once in a while. This will help clear up RAM, make your computer run more efficient, and keep the battery refreshed.

iCloud

iOS users may already be familiar with iCloud since it's one of the first things that you are asked to create, but if you are new to the Apple ecosystem, iCloud is Apple's cloud-based storage solution. You may be thinking, "What the heck does that mumbo jumbo mean?" The best way to think about the cloud is an invisible storage center that is everywhere and nowhere at the same time. You can upload data to store on it, and access the data at any given time on another device without taking up space since it is stored elsewhere. There are many different cloud storage systems like iCloud including Dropbox and SugarSync, but iCloud does things a little differently.

- You'll be able to backup your contacts so they are synced perfectly across your Mac, iPhone, iPad, and iPod. Make a change in a contact card or add a new contact, and the change or addition will be reflected across all of your synced iCloud devices.

- The addition of Google Drive allows you to store all kinds of files and documents that can be accessed by most devices that can connect to the web, not just Apple devices.

- Signing up for iCloud will net you a free 5 GB of storage.

- Media files purchased through the iTunes Store won't count against your storage.

If you haven't set up an iCloud account, you can create one by going to System Preferences > iCloud and following the on screen instructions. Once you're finished, you'll be able to select what kind of data you'd like synced through iCloud: Photos, Mail, Contacts, Calendars, Safari, Notes, Keychain, and more. At the bottom you will notice a bar that indicates how much storage has been used up, and how much available storage you have left.

Owning all Apple products can be a beautiful thing, but if you are using multiple iCloud accounts things could get hairy and ugly very quickly. It's good practice to maintain a single iCloud account across your Apple devices to have the information synced up perfectly unless you absolutely need to have another one for some reason.

Loving iCloud but need more storage? You can purchase more room by going to System Preferences > iCloud, and in the bottom right corner click on Manage. The Manage Storage window will come up, and in the top right you can select Buy More Storage. The following storage plans are currently available:

- 20 GB for $0.99 a month

iCloud

iOS users may already be familiar with iCloud since it's one of the first things that you are asked to create, but if you are new to the Apple ecosystem, iCloud is Apple's cloud-based storage solution. You may be thinking, "What the heck does that mumbo jumbo mean?" The best way to think about the cloud is an invisible storage center that is everywhere and nowhere at the same time. You can upload data to store on it, and access the data at any given time on another device without taking up space since it is stored elsewhere. There are many different cloud storage systems like iCloud including Dropbox and SugarSync, but iCloud does things a little differently.

- You'll be able to backup your contacts so they are synced perfectly across your Mac, iPhone, iPad, and iPod. Make a change in a contact card or add a new contact, and the change or addition will be reflected across all of your synced iCloud devices.

- The addition of Google Drive allows you to store all kinds of files and documents that can be accessed by most devices that can connect to the web, not just Apple devices.

- Signing up for iCloud will net you a free 5 GB of storage.

- Media files purchased through the iTunes Store won't count against your storage.

If you haven't set up an iCloud account, you can create one by going to System Preferences > iCloud and following the on screen instructions. Once you're finished, you'll be able to select what kind of data you'd like synced through iCloud: Photos, Mail, Contacts, Calendars, Safari, Notes, Keychain, and more. At the bottom you will notice a bar that indicates how much storage has been used up, and how much available storage you have left.

Owning all Apple products can be a beautiful thing, but if you are using multiple iCloud accounts things could get hairy and ugly very quickly. It's good practice to maintain a single iCloud account across your Apple devices to have the information synced up perfectly unless you absolutely need to have another one for some reason.

Loving iCloud but need more storage? You can purchase more room by going to System Preferences > iCloud, and in the bottom right corner click on Manage. The Manage Storage window will come up, and in the top right you can select Buy More Storage. The following storage plans are currently available:

- 20 GB for $0.99 a month

- 200 GB for $3.99 a month
- 500 GB for $9.99 a month
- 1 TB for $19.99 a month

If you decide to change your mind and don't need the extra storage plans, Apple gives you 15 days to contact them and ask for a refund.

Conclusion

With OS X Yosemite, Apple has proved once again that it is highly skilled at designing with the user experience in mind. While the looks may be different than previous OS X versions, the new appearance will help close the gap between iOS devices and Macs, in turn reducing the learning curve for users. Now that you know a thing or two about the fancy gadget in front of you, it's time to put that knowledge to use! Get out there and have fun.

CPSIA information can be obtained
at www.ICGtesting.com
Printed in the USA
LVOW04s0956010516
486170LV00044B/681/P